THE 8 KEYS
TO SUCCESSFUL LIVING

Published by BASSUAH PUBLISHING LIMITED, London.

The information in this book is intended to be educational and not for the diagnosis, prescription or treatment of any health disorder. The author and publisher are not liable for any misuse of this material and the information presented.

A CIP Catalogue record for this book is available from the British Library.

ISBN - 978-1-9160283-1-9
ISBN - 978-1-9160283-0-2

ACKNOWLEDGEMENT

The author wishes to say a special thanks to the following for their love, support and inspiration:

Christina Konadu
Felix Bassuah
Fidelis Bassuah
Felix Bassuah Jnr
Grace Bassuah
Lili Shi
Sandra Brutkoski

DEDICATION

This book is dedicated to Our Protectors and to the entirety of the one and only Human race on this planet, a race with a rich diversity that has for so long been wrongfully divided.

PREFACE

The aim of this book is to aid you in understanding and seeing yourself as a source of great dynamic power, a power that has always been available for your use, to recreate your world for the better. The laid out KEYS in this book are to act as a guide, helping you through the journey of self-discovery and to help you see success under a new and better light. The principles revealed in this book helps you in identifying your mind as a key entity and the only basis on which any concept of success in the human world can be realised. Reading and understanding this book will empower you to successfully bridge the enormous and seemingly impossible gap that exists between your dreams and your reality.

Just as I found, and many others have found, my wish and desire for you is that you too can also come to realise that the old enormous and overwhelming gap that has denied you your dreams and full expression of your life all this time is a temporary, artificial construct. Thankfully, this temporary artificial construct can be overpowered and eliminated once you know how and act on the relevant set of principles. As you make this extraordinary journey through this book, you will come to see that with the right mindset and right actions, nothing will be impossible to you.

When a thing or an idea is revealed to you (alone), it ceases to be mysterious to you (alone). Therefore, take heed to the words of wisdom you are reading, to avoid encountering the same fate as the many men and women, who throughout history have fallen prematurely and become victims of strange circumstances and corrupt simulations.

For over 2000 years, have you noticed that the popularly accepted and trending success definitions have been misleading and incomplete at best? However, since success is something worthy of pursuing, many innocent people have lost their self-worth, their nature, sanctity and their sense in pursuing an artificial status that society hails as success. Before you is the KEY to end this deception.

The 8 KEYS TO SUCCESSFUL LIVING is a great literary masterpiece that has come at such a time as this, to usher you into your inalienable destiny of abundance, a meaningful purpose and perpetual glory, without the unthinkable wastage, unreasonable sacrifices, betrayal and compromises that have long since been held as the norm. You deserve more and you deserve better!

Over the last twenty centuries, the continuous mis-education and dissemination of lies, has created a new breed of individuals who have become so disconnected from their source and from nature, and become so distant to the affairs of (human) life. They have altogether become highly sensitive and responsive to superficial, hollow and insignificant matters of life and in contrast they have become highly insensitive and unresponsive to great, meaningful and significant matters of life. This is a condition you must do your best to avoid at all costs.

Success is one of the most talked about concepts and yet least practiced concept in the world today. The road of success is one of the most famous and often talked about roads but the least travelled road in the world today. Majority of human beings today have fallen into the habit of automatically or subconsciously taking for granted the fundamental two-fold nature of what it means to be successful as a person. More on this will be outlined later in the second KEY. We often talk about success in an emotional or materialistic sense, either ignoring, or totally being unconscious to the essential precondition necessary to enable one to recognise success or to be recognised as being successful.

This compact manual is the secret, the push, that empowerment, that spark you have been waiting for all this while. Receive it with all diligence and adhere to all that it contains in the strictest sense, with all your might, will and ability. This manual before you is pragmatic, not philosophical.

The body is the temple of the Supreme Energy (or in modern terms 'God') within you; and so it is said: *know-thyself*. This book acts not only as a seal breaker but also as a template on the subject of success, unveiling hidden mysteries and offering you uninhibited access to a more holistic, complete success as a human being and how to attain this rare state of life that has eluded many humans till now.

This book has been carefully written to accommodate all readers and be as politically correct as can be when presenting verifiable truth in a system characterised by complex lies that perpetuates injustice and the 'financially profitable' but unnecessary bloodsheds under the deceptive yet popular slogan of 'Working Together For The Greater Good Of All Mankind'.

Contents

KEY 1: UNDERSTANDING THE BUSINESS OF DEFINING SUCCESS

"To know about others and your surrounding is to demonstrate existence, but to know yourself, is to demonstrate the essence of life and to truly live."

Finbarr Bassuah

1.0 Understanding The Secret In Plain Sight

Once upon a time, all you knew was all you knew until…! Now all you will know and all you are confident in, and all you will be proud of and protect is understandably, everything you were taught, and that which you know.

So it is expected that you will automatically trigger a 'learned' reaction and quick response in defence of what you know and are aware of all your life once you get any new knowledge, message or hear something new that is not in your circle of awareness. This will include resisting or challenging any information or knowledge new to you and not in your current belief system. You may even feel that your personality and culture is being attacked by the incoming new information you are not aware of and you may have all kinds of emotions including anger and fear welling up inside you. But try your best to calm yourself down, take slow deep breaths and listen to that new information without overreacting or being too overwhelmed with emotions. These are all part of the process of mental development and personal development.

To grow, you have to become something you were not before, or else you cannot say that you have grown. And in the same way, to become successful (in whatever capacity and endeavour) you need to do something you have never done before, and become something you have never been before. Such is the process of change and growth. Therefore, you need to manage it well to your advantage. Your time of favour and liberation has come.

"SPACE - (by Felix Bassuah)

I was once asleep, till that great awakening caused by
the thundering sound of the trumpet.
The trumpet of the saviour
Warping that old grim and false existence I knew as
reality.
Then behold, I saw a new world.
I saw the Space; and the meaning it emitted all
around.

I never imagined that just one simple awareness and
understanding of a concept can open up a whole new
and amazing world.

So now I fully understand
That it was the Space between each iron bar that
held the mighty lion captive.
The rows of spaces between those bars held back the
mighty Lion.
Now I see how that mighty Lion King was held back.
Just as the refusal to think holds back freedom,
development, and the full expression of life itself.

It is the same Space that exists between the notes
which makes up the music I have always loved
listening to.
And now I see that the same Space, which acts as
pauses between the sounds and notes, makes up
those wonderful melodies to which I dance every
other day.

It is the same Space between these walls that makes a
home
And not the walls I always see around me each time
I am home.
I am home when I am within that Space of
splendour.

With that being said, the Space in the glass jar forms
what I call a beautiful glass jar.
Now see as this glass jar perfectly holds in place that
refreshing and nutritious fruit juice
Holding beautifully the drink I love to enjoy with my
family on a hot sunny day.

In this revelation, it becomes clear that each Space
within the fence together makes up the tennis court
on which I always play that wonderful game of
tennis.
And that large, well defined Space within the
spectacular structure is the stadium we gather for
football and other sports or social activities.

How then could I have missed all this?
And for what purpose?
My existence has for so long to this day been
regulated by this same Space principle.
Yet I was oblivious to the existence of Space's reality.

Even the wonderfully formed spaces on my very own
skin all over my body serve as a covering
A protection and a barrier preventing dangerous
substances from entering my body.
A protection I failed to reverence.

These wonderful and magnificent spaces on my skin
act as a natural protective barrier
Allowing the excretion of toxins and sweat, while
intelligently absorbing into my body vital elements
from the atmosphere
And absorbing the wonderful atmospheric energy
and vitamins from the sun.

How incredible, to be blinded to Space for so long.
To be blinded to such display of majesty.
So be it, better late than never!
At last reality is unveiled
And I have once again become a living being living
in that Space in truth and harmony."

Success is one of the most talked about concepts and yet the least practiced concepts in the world today. The road of success is one of the most famous and often talked about road but the least travelled road in this postmodern age. The aim of this book is to change the whole dynamics on the topic and understanding of success and delve into depths that have hitherto been unknown.

We find ourselves in a rather strange world of inconceivable, enormous competition, accelerated change and overwhelming complexity. However, can you confirm with absolute certainty, that this undesirable and unhealthy competitive global state of the current world we know is the true state and reflection of the original, natural world we ought to live in? Absolutely not. This will become clearer as we go on further into this matter.

We are as humans living in a world called earth, with unimaginable abundance of resources and yet we somehow manage to get caught up in enormous, fierce competition at all levels of society and existence. Famine is destroying cities, ending countless lives, while food wastage and disposal is a mass problem among many nations. Some communities are ravaged with famine and drought while neighbouring communities few miles or few kilometres away are so well fed that they have problems disposing large surpluses they classify as wastage daily. The USA is a classic example of this aforementioned situation, although it is not the only nation guilty of such waste and disparity.

Instead of creative thinking and diving into the potential mental power at our disposable, people have quietly come to the common agreement to settle for less, in their comfort zones, crippled with fear, following the crowd and drawing their identity from the Masses. This has led to the creation of what some may call the 'Me Too' society, filled with 'Me Too' generations, repeating the same mistakes over and over again.

In such a society, many will do anything for success, risking their lives and using all kinds of immoral, genocidal, tyrannical, inhumane and dubious ways to achieve material gains and economic power (which they see and define as success), while losing themselves and their dignity in the process of chasing after this fallacy and illusion they wrongfully identify as success. So in the end, all that is left is a regretful, bitter, soulless society of individuals filled with shame and despair, fuelled with greed, in an attempt at achieving what they believed to be "success".

All things considered, to be yourself is the best principle for any honest individual. This is because you really have no other choice than to be yourself, to represent yourself, especially if you want to maintain the right to be unique.

Moreover, you have no choice in becoming anyone else you admire because that admirer you would like to be or impersonate has already been taken, occupied by the original owner living in that body which you so admire. So it would appear you are too late. take heart, for all hope is not lost. You still have one option: to be yourself. To be or not to be, that is something you have to answer directly or indirectly, and there is no way of avoiding that. Anyway, it is very unlikely that you would admire and consider an impersonator, a fraud and a deceiver as a role model from which you draw inspiration, and rightly so. This lesson is important because it deals with the foundations of what it means to be human. This move can then protect the essence of the value of your human life from being reduced to nothing more than 'a battle of survival of the fittest'.

Survival of the fittest is nothing more than a politically coded philosophy to justify the evil and uncivilised ways of creating riches by any means necessary, whether it may be through forced slavery, oppressions, genocides, wars, terrorism and imperialism. We should rather strive to live together as one human family in the spirit of harmony, in cooperation and prosperity as we grow and develop together.

If an alien (a Martian) for example was to take up residence on earth and become the richest being in this world through the creation of a successful tech company, what would you refer to this alien as? Would this alien be known as the richest businessman or person in the world?

Surely we cannot say he is the most successful alien because this alien is living in a world of humans, so this title of the most successful alien would make no sense. Let us leave that illustration there for now. Therefore, it is imperative to establish your identity or have full knowledge of who you are before you can lay claim to any legitimate success.

The manual presented before you will delve into depths that have hitherto been unknown and untouched in relation to the existing public discourse about (human) success. The 8 KEYS TO SUCCESSFUL LIVING will empower the reader to become more equipped and capable at translating their ideals or dreams into tangible reality. By studying and understanding this manual and carefully following the principles and instructions laid out before you, the achievement and manifestation of those noble desires you seek is guaranteed. The main aim of this first KEY is to lay the right foundation and understanding on which the following KEYS will be developed.

Committing yourself fully to understanding these KEYS, together with your strong desire for liberation and a meaningful, rich life will ensure your victory. Remember that where there is a will, there is a way. A mind once expanded can never contract or shrink, and therein lies the dilemma of freedom or finding yourself. Freedom whether it be an illusionist concept or a real concept is something dear that has to be gained or taken. Freedom is not a gift to be offered to you simply because you deserve or have a right to it, for if it were so, everyone would have freedom. Again if this were so, few wars, no terrorist acts and no freedom fighters would exist in this current world as all those sincerely and legitimately seeking freedom would have attained it and there would be no need for terrorism, bloodshed, or any form of armed conflict, all in the attempt of pursuing freedom and justice. No one in their right mind would go through the painstaking trouble of taking away your freedom for any reason they may have just so they can turn around and give it to you simply because you deserve it or they turned over a new leaf.

When you get an offer that opens up possibilities and ways for the attainment of your liberation, do all you can to take it and run with it, because that is the only sure way your circumstance will change, and the only way by which you can grab your freedom. After attaining your freedom, do well to keep it and refrain from that addictive habit of getting stuck in a perpetual struggle for your freedom or liberation. The following KEYS will show you just how to do that and more.

1.1 Standard And Trending Definitions Of Success

Presented below is a general overview of the popular and mostly accepted definitions of success and how it is currently understood and taught all over the world to date.

In modern society, success is often summarised in these three words or a combination of any or all of the three:

> 1.MONEY
> 2.POWER/FAME
> 3.HAPPINESS.

Some dictionaries define success as the attainment or accomplishment of an aim or purpose.

According to Webster's dictionary, success is defined as the fact of achieving wealth or respect.

Whether unconsciously or consciously, people in general, that is most people or otherwise referred to as the Masses, have long since been conditioned and educated through various multiple institutions and mediums to equate success to power, money and happiness. This may involve a conditioning process to accept either of the three, a combination of the three or all of the three pillars upon which the current global definition of (human) success hangs: Money, Power/Fame and Happiness. Others may go further and add such things as freedom of choice, expression or independence in defining or understanding what success is.

A word of caution to readers:
The definitions below in their entirety apply only to those individuals speaking (and their family and friends), members of their brotherhood, cult, or those individuals at their level of wealth and influence and in no way applies to you regardless of how sincere and passionate they may sound in delivering you such a message/philosophy. Let us apply some critical thinking skills to this issue to dispel any misunderstanding. That so-called 'success' reality they are pushing on you by logic can never be your reality and you are sadly being sold empty promises and unattainable hope unless they handpick you into their circle of wealth and influence, or unless you are a relative to those speakers quoted below and the groups pushing such agendas. You do not need to agree or disagree with this statement, but as you keep reading diligently, all will become clear sooner than you expected.

Let us now look at several reports on what some of the world's richest men, including those on Forbes rich list, and some famous teachers and personalities have said or taught on the subject of success. Bill Gates, the owner of Microsoft Windows, is the second wealthiest person in the world behind Jeff Bezos. According to a report by the Business Insider online, Bill Gates explains that success is about relationships and leaving behind a legacy. The Business Insider article continues to explain that in a previous interview, Bill Gates took a tip from Warren Buffett when asked about his definition of success. "Warren Buffett has always said the measure [of success] is whether the people close to you are happy and love you." He added: "It is also nice to feel like you made a difference — inventing something or raising kids or helping people in need."

Billionaire investor Mark Cuban says "To me, the definition of success is waking up in the morning with a smile on your face, knowing it's going to be a great day. I was happy and felt like I was successful when I was poor, living six guys in a three-bedroom apartment, sleeping on the floor".

According to Richard Branson, founder of the Virgin Group, worth some $5 billion, "Too many people measure how successful they are by how much money they make or the people that they associate with," he wrote on LinkedIn. "In my opinion, true success should be measured by how happy you are." Spiritual teacher, and author Deepak Chopra believes success is a matter of constant growth. According to the Indian teacher, "Success in life could be defined as the continued expansion of happiness and the progressive realisation of worthy goals.".

While all these and many other definitions could be given to explain success and what it means to be a successful individual, these statements or definitions do not measure up to what it means to be a successful human and most of all, they are just too ambiguous.

The obvious problem with such inadequate, yet standardised and accepted definitions is that, on their own, these definitions may be said to be true for some people and not true for others depending on the society, family fortunes and environment within which individuals were raised among other factors. Yet it is meant to be a definition pertaining to humanity and success of individuals belong to that human family or human species.

Each definition seems incomplete upon analysis. Through different perspectives you can see a strange phenomenon arise, and this is the fact that the core of the definition of what it means to be a successful individual is missing in the given definitions above. This is true for all other literature and popular publications circulating the globe today.

In fact, the man with the wealthiest family in the history of America to date, John D. Rockefeller once said that "It is wrong to assume that men of immense wealth are always happy". Attributed as a statement to his Bible class (1 April 1905) in "The Loneliness of John D. Rockefeller", *Current Literature* (November 1906) vol. 41 no. 5)".

Does this mean those successful, happy people cease to be successful once their happiness is gone since happiness is taught as a definition for what it means to be a successful person.

For those who may not know about this family, the Rockefeller's created a special board called the General Education Board in the USA in 1902 and the aim of this board was the promotion of education throughout the United States. After a successful implementation, the old style of voluntary education was abolished and a new system of compulsory education was introduced for all American citizens with the backing of the American government. The newly created system of compulsory education by the Rockefeller General Education Board was then spread worldwide with the funding and under the direction of the Rockefeller family.

As you read on, you may begin to see that we may have taken some things for granted and that things don't seem to add up on popular and trending conversations on the topic of human success. By critically observing what is said to be the standard for success, one can begin to see that success in relation to humans is not simply an attainment of a desired object or material as it has been taught for the last 2,000 years. Rather, success can be seen as a precursor to human development and achievements.

"I don't want a nation of thinkers, I want a nation of workers"- attributed to John D. Rockefeller.

Concluding statement: Free your mind, Free yourself.

KEY 2: RIGHT KNOWLEDGE AND YOU

"Actually hard work is good and indeed necessary, but in all your workings, remember to live."

Felix Bassuah

2.0 A Holistic Definition Of A Successful Person

This second KEY gives an objective and holistic definition of what it means to be a successful individual. Further discussion is made to include the various aspects of success as a concept and all matters relating to the understanding of the topic of success and its attainment.

Definition of Success: Success or being a successful person is being born anew, knowing what you are, coupled with understanding your environment and rightly relating to your kind (fellow humans) and your environment in harmony.

The hallmark of becoming successful is when you are able to positively impact the world around you with the investments of your personality.

Further explanation on the various parts of being born again (anew) will be discussed further in this second KEY and references will also be made in the other KEYS to follow. The above definition of Success can be best described as a two-fold definition. The first part of the success definition refers to (the process of) being born anew, knowing what you are, who you are, and being that which you are. The second and final part of this definition is (the process of) understanding your environment and rightly relating to your kind and your environment in harmony.

By expanding the above definition in a global context, we are presented with two major components, that is, two big 'C's, namely Creation and Cooperation.

Creation here involves not only the creation and continuous recreation of one's self but also involves bringing into the physical plane great and noble inventions that propels and fuels the development of human society. Here you can see creation as bringing into being that which is not yet physically present through the help and guide of directed and focused mental activity besides any other forms of activity that may facilitate the process of creation. This form of creation also encompasses procreation or the continuity of your lineage through giving birth.

We can liken recreation to getting or undergoing an upgrade as we see in terms of computers, smart phones, or other electronic gadgets undergoing upgrades. These electronic gadgets undergo upgrades which allow them to function at higher, faster rates or spectrums and process much more data or information than they could have processed previously under the old models.

Through such upgrades, they end up undergoing remodelling or servicing with better security, protection and improved features with dynamic, robust operating systems and interfaces that can compensate for unexpected future eventualities. Above all, such upgrades extend the life span of that equipment, gadget or artificial intelligence besides the boost in performance. This form of upgrade rightly describes what we gain from the art of creation and the recreation process we undergo through mind renewal or mind transformation.

The second 'C' being Cooperation encompasses relations and relationship building, teamwork or unity towards the realisation of worthy goals and effective communication. This second C is all about living in harmony with one's self, relatives and friends, and the community or nation in which you live.

On a more cosmic level, this state of Cooperation will involve the individual progressing from his or her oneness with herself, family and friends to becoming one with the world or universe in which they live. This is a part of returning to your source and origin. Only by getting in that original state can you be at your best and perform above mediocrity.

Nature, which is omnipotent, was here long before you came into this world and will be here long after you are gone. Any attempt to conquer Nature is a show of vanity and will only lead to anguish, despair, and eventually your self destruction or your extinction.

Having explained what success entails for every human alive today, it is now proper to address the issue of 'Competition' at this point. There is no arena or basis for introducing a third 'C' (Competition) of any sort in this already complete and holistic definition. The third 'C' will through things out of balance and do more harm than good. Since this given definition with its two complimentary halves is self-sustaining, there is in fact no necessity for introducing any form of competition whether it is the so-called healthy competition or unhealthy competition. If we don't actively come together to put an end to this mind-games what do you suppose would be labelled healthy next: a healthy racism, healthy discrimination or healthy rape? surely at this is nothing more than a game of semantics and we belonging to the human race or species should not become victims and slaves of such mindless games and auto-suggestions.

The secret of the matter is that competition itself is detrimental to you, whichever form it may come. So be very careful not to make the mistake of accepting "competition" as a necessary part of your life. Remember that competition is a sin. In fact, permit me to reveal more hidden secrets relating to cosmic or universal laws so you can see the damage competition causes to you directly and indirectly.

By living in an arena of competition or accepting and practicing the concept of competition, whether you call it a healthy competition or an unhealthy one, you automatically fall down to a lower plane of existence. In that lower plane of existence and life, you find that everything is now about surviving and you grind; you hustle and bustle, and struggle for survival in the world of survivors, under the law of survival of the fittest and in this case there is no way you can flourish and excel until you are out of that plane of fierce and unholy competition. This fierce competitiveness and other violent modes of survival leads to the gradual acceptance of the lethal philosophies and practices of survival by any means necessary, which spirals uncontrollably into all manner of greed and evil.

In fact, you are far more capable, with unimaginable potential deposited within you and the members of your entire body than you have been taught. So why get stuck in a field of competitiveness? Growth, development and creation are all independent of competition and all great and significant achievements of men and women throughout the records of human histories have been purely out of creation and cooperation.

Fierce competition only produces a chain reaction of hypertension for its practitioners, cardiac arrests and chronic stress, the practice of cutting corners, making ridiculously unholy gains/profits, creating economic depressions and suicides and armed conflicts. So ask yourself if you really need to continue on the destructive path of accelerated competition and fierce competitiveness all of which you were raised to believe was a necessity in your life and quest for success. Competitiveness is the grandmother of greed (for power, wealth, riches and so on). And by now I am sure we all know a thing or two about what happens to the greedy and those with insatiable and unchecked appetite.

2.1 No Success Until You Be Born Again

I have simplified this holistic and concise definition above for easy assimilation. It will be a great advantage for you to re-visit the definition of success given here as many times as possible until it is embedded on the tablet of your heart and in your mind so as not to miss out on the immense benefit and power it contains. This definition is not simply a statement of being yourself. Assuming that would be a total misunderstanding of the definition presented here. For if success were that easy to understand and attain, there would not be that many unsuccessful individuals, with many existing variations and contradictory teachings and concepts on the definition of what it means to be a successful person.

This kind of polarisation and wrongful teachings on the subject of success has contributed greatly to the evils of society especially with the case of the ever growing income inequality gap between the rich and the poor in society. All the lovely speeches and lip service of equality, freedom, justice and global agendas to fight poverty, slavery, abuse, diseases and terrorism are sharply contrasted and abruptly halted by the current existing reality of high inequality gaps, high rewards and incentives for illegitimate leaders and tyrants and growth of extreme injustice.

According to a Bloomberg article on global wealth published in November 2017, the gap between rich and poor may be reaching its peak. The article says that analysts at the Swiss bank's Research Institute said "In recent years, wealth inequality has trended upwards". The article also warns that "Income inequality has become a hot-button issue since the crisis, with economists warning that it is polarizing society and stoking discontent."

Another report by the World Economic Forum in 2017 stated that "The gap between rich and poor has increased in almost every region of the world over the last four decades". That means such systemic inequality is not a national problem for us in the UK alone or in America alone, but an existing global issue, although it has not received the proper attention and redress it deserves, just like ignoring or pretending to notice the huge elephant in the room, hoping by ignoring it, that huge elephant will somehow have no impact or cause any ruckus and in due time will conveniently disappear into thin air. "In January, the World Economic Forum (WEF) found rising income inequality and the polarization of sectors in societies ranked among key underlying trends likely to shape the world over the next decade. The WEF's global risks report also said the widening gap between rich and poor was behind U.S. President Donald Trump's election victory and the U.K.'s Brexit vote."

These misunderstandings on the subject of success underpins the common phenomenon where the story of success for one individual within a particular society is considered a complete, abysmal failure by his or her neighbour across the street or in that same community. After all, if humans were one as a species and possessed a comprehensive understanding of what it means to be human, then where from the multitude of extremely polarised and contradictory statements and definitions on the single subject of being a successful person?

For clarity and escaping from all the intellectual fallacy and confusing opinions, go back and re-read the holistic definition of success given, repeatedly, till you are familiar with each word, phrase and completely understand the definition. This will serve as a barrier or protector, shielding you away from any conspiracies and systematic lies or falsified historical and scientific accounts aimed at taking power from you (the believer, student or recipient) and transferring it to the false giver and deceiver.

All things are in constant motion and thus it behoves you to move forward if you are to thrive and develop. By being productive, you can maintain a brighter, prosperous, and more independent future. It is important to know your history as you begin the journey of self-discovery, and this is because everything (a result) has a cause and nothing occurs by chance. In fact, what many refer to as chance in life is actually a name for a Law not known or recognised and nothing escapes that Law.

Knowing yourself and understanding yourself, your environment and how best to interact with your outside world is the definition of the real and lasting success for every living human as established earlier. We can also see this achievement as the unshakable foundation upon which all other (human) accomplishments, great and small, are attained, and celebrated accordingly.

Upon achieving self-knowledge, you gain mastery of yourself and enter a supernatural state of harmony where you become one with your internal world and your external world. You will know the right individuals to associate with, what to look for, when and how to act and operate including many other things such as what and how to prioritise everything in your daily life, in the management of your time, efforts and life. So without a question, you need to know your history, and the journey, including the events that has created and shaped you into your current state, to see and make the right decisions for any necessary steps to be taken. Those who have lost the knowledge of their past are doomed to repeat all the avoidable mistakes of the past.

Knowing your purpose will be easier once you are one and in tune with the universal force that animates and sustains you. In this state, things will fall in their right and proper place concerning you and you will naturally attract that which is appropriate for you and your purpose will gravitate towards you as you develop affinity one for another. In this state, you become master of the self and are no longer subject to the heavy sway of external emotions and so on.

You will lose your previously gained lifestyle of being a struggling survivor and a victim, and become a new being, with new privileges including the privileges of a victor. You are no longer a lost sheep or a lost individual; you are no longer a sinner in need of redemption or salvation; you are no longer an ignorant person being tossed from one side to the other by a multitude of doctrines and philosophies. You become a new creature, old things have in fact passed away and behold, all things become new, as you come into the new dimension of a new life and existence. On this level of existence and in this new plane of life, you become the able director of your fate and co-creator with the one true

Creative force, Universal/infinite mind or the God that exists.

This is that elevated and mysterious state that many individuals are consciously or unconsciously yearning for, whether they be politicians, political leaders, superstars, businessmen and women, spiritual leaders, religious leaders, teachers, monks, gurus and so on. This is the quintessential state of being a successful human being on this planet or in any world in which you live. This is the only suitable and natural foundation for any other common or extraordinary achievement or endeavours that any human may attain.

Until you are you, there is nothing you can do in your capacity as YOU, yourself. There is no denying this simple declaration of truth. This is the reality and there is no argument, no opinion or way around this simple statement of fact and truth. It is the reality we are to deal with. It is either to be or not to be, either you are you or you are not you and nothing in-between. Once you learn to be yourself and become yourself (again), you will stand in self-knowledge and shed away all unnecessary weights that once held you in bondage. By this unveiling, you will know and identify what works for you and what does not work for you. Once you know yourself, you will see where you came from, where you have been, where you are, and ultimately where you ought to go or be.

2.2 We Disclose To The Wise Ones In Proverbs

Some say that wisdom, is a protection even as money is a protection, but the excellent advantage of wisdom over money is that wisdom shields and preserves the lives of its possessors. So even if you had money for such protection, it would require wisdom or knowledge to make this happen as you make the right choices for implementation. Money comes with it so much unimaginable troubles, a heightened sense of many sane and insane adventures, and not forgetting the many fake friends that riches draw to us. Therefore, individuals who have both money (in large amounts) and wisdom often state that wisdom has the upper hand on money in matters of life and security.

With the analysis and presentations in this book, understanding the definition of success will automatically position you and equip you in attaining complete, lasting success in life without compromising on security, meaningful times and deeper satisfaction of body, soul and mind.

For your sake, I will cover all things necessary to giving you a fulfilled life without worry and without compromise. In fact, success as presented here will be an ever growing and ever expanding one as you will eventually come to bear witness to, as long as you are genuine in your endeavours. This understanding will help you see a world beyond achieving annual goals or new year resolutions. You can then position yourself for a more beautiful life beyond the attainment of short-lasting, perishable materials and move into a life of lasting values and principles, joy, fulfilment and the creation of a lasting legacy long after you are no longer available physically.

The most important part of the concept of success is not about the quantity of material gains that one can possess. The acquisition of material things and riches are noteworthy achievements but these are only a fraction of the results you should look out for in the life of any successful person. Being successful, again, truly has nothing to do with getting large amounts of currency in your possession or landing a good job you have always wanted, although these may be a part of the results that comes with living life as a successful individual.

We can acknowledge the importance of currency or money in current societies since it has the power as a tool and resource to enable you to achieve many goals in life. However, if money alone could be counted as a measure for success, then perhaps it would be impossible for anyone who was rich or had lots of money to have regrets in life or give up their entire riches in search of meaning or a new purpose for their life as we have witnessed many multi-millionaires do.

It is common knowledge and a common headline in newspapers and on social media that millionaires and billionaires in parts of USA, Europe, Asia and around the world commit suicide, leaving behind their millions of dollars or Euros in their bank accounts. Thus, riches alone, as already established, is not the hallmark or definition of success. It is a noteworthy by-product of being a successful person alongside other by-products such as good relations and so on.

Again, success is not primarily about getting a family of your own or getting married. If that were so, there would be no divorce in the world because why would you want to divorce and break that symbol or throw away that achievement you call success by getting a divorce? Yet as we all know, there are many, unending number of divorces and marital problems which has resulted in the divorce courts and divorce lawyers being among the top earning lawyers globally, especially in the Americas and parts of Europe. Besides this, family disputes and lawsuits among family members and the huge sums of settlements have become another line of a booming business.

The most important part of the success equation is something I call the "YOU" factor. Perhaps this is one of the greatest secrets hidden from the inhabitants of this planet earth. Without understanding 'you' (yourself), there is and there can be no true success for you as an individual. If someone told you anything different, then either you misunderstood what was being said or you were lied to. You cannot become a successful you if you yourself are outside that success equation, just like you quench your thirst by drinking water yourself, and not by having someone drink water on your behalf to quench the thirst you have.

Without knowing yourself, all you may do is setting targets and meeting those targets, and this is no special achievement. This is because all kinds of animals both smart animals and dumb animals from the intelligent dolphins to unintelligent dodos and pandas, all meet their targets and achieve their set goals daily, whether it be entertaining guests by playing volleyball with trainers in a pool or eating some food or chewing on some bamboo shoots and making more baby dolphins or baby pandas.

You are literally the embodiment of the most essential factor in the human success equation that has either been deliberately omitted or eluded our experts and philosophers for millennia. This has left many individuals in society on a wild goose chase.

It doesn't matter how much you pray, fast, or believe in some divine power to make you successful. This is wishful thinking, nothing more than a simple case of folly or naivety because there has been no concrete historical evidence or contemporary evidence to support such claims of attaining success through the likes of fasting or prayers in any part of the world. If it were so, Africa for example, which is the most religious continent on the planet and has the highest number of practicing Christians and churches in the world, would be the most successful part of the world. Yet Africa is plagued with much corruption and unimaginable suffering such as great famine/hunger, armed conflicts and poverty right in the land of great natural resources, precious stones and vast plantations of many kinds of crops.

2.3 'You' Were 'The Secret' All Along

The constant elusiveness of the state, called success, can only be realised once you get to know yourself and be yourself. Here is a worthy question to ponder over: How can you be successful without yourself or without your being? How can you (inserting your name here) become successful without knowing your true identity and self? You are no more, more human than the first day you were born and named.

After your birth, you naturally begin an evolutionary process of growth and development, where you progressively move into adulthood. Success follows this same pattern. You become successful and then grow in success. This will involve you growing and developing on a success-based foundation. Ideally, you become successful as a human being once in your lifetime, and that is when real life begins for you as an individual. This is the rebirth you experience, the second birth you must go through as you grow in the right knowledge of self (yourself).

The other things you lay claim to and label as 'success' are the natural and expected manifestations of your coming into existence as a complete (successful) human being. These material gains can at best be described as fitting attachments to the essence of success. So, for example, the invention of technology or new machines you create will be the physical, tangible outworking of your new and uninhibited mind as a person, empowering you in creating those inventions and so on. It is that same well-developed mind of yours that helps you in completing whatever task or aim worthy of accomplishing as a human.

Too often we see many teachers, journalists and celebrities or superstars teaching or spreading a fundamental misunderstanding and misconceptions on the meaning of what it means to be a successful individual. After decades and generations of being born and raised into these lies and misunderstandings, or half-truths, many innocent individuals have developed obligations and strong emotional attachments to these lies, half-truths and mis-educations. A common example of such popular misunderstanding or misconception is equating being a successful human to the mere accomplishment of set targets or goals.

Strictly speaking, you are not a successful human because you achieved your new year resolution of losing 10 pounds in body weight in half a year or reaching your target savings of two million dollars within the five year time-frame you set yourself. Completing a formal school education and graduating with a certificate does not suddenly make you a successful human either. Achieving your goal of being able to swim the distance of one mile in five minutes alone does not automatically transform you into a successful human. These things at best can be classed as the (successful) completion of set targets. Any other individual could equally complete these targets easily without your involvement. So you cannot claim success outside of yourself or outside your very own nature and identity.

Now you wouldn't go around celebrating and calling a dolphin a successful dolphin because it could learn how to play indoor volley ball or other ball games in a pool with some dolphin trainers in an aquarium or amusement park. These sea creatures raised and trained for entertainment and amusement at ocean parks and aquariums to play ball or jump through hoops and do some back flips to entertain viewers cannot be labelled or described as successful dolphins because of their ability to play ball and follow orders from trainers. These dolphins or sea creatures playing ball and following trainers on entertainment routines are acting outside their nature and are out of character. Therefore, they cannot be portrayed as or held in esteem and celebrated as successful dolphins or sea creatures.

Most dolphins who live freely in their natural habitats in the depths of the oceans cannot be said to be unsuccessful because they do not know how to play ball games or entertain tourists at ocean parks or amusement parks. Such activities are not the normal or natural endeavours a dolphin ought to embark on and this life of a well-trained, captive dolphin is not the wish or dream of any dolphin; to be captured and forced into training daily to perform for the entertainment of others and make money for their masters and trainers who are keeping them in captivity. They are perfect and successful, and are exactly where they are supposed to be, in the sea, doing and being exactly what they ought to do and be, sea creatures. That is success. Only humans seem to have a problem with this natural phenomenon and cosmic logic.

Therefore, it is understandable that being able to do these things does not imply that these captured sea creatures are successful sea creatures because they can play indoor ball games well or jump through hoops. That is because these signs are not the hallmarks of being a dolphin or a sea creature. It only shows their ability to learn or do something under coercion. The same goes for humans also, that is the ability to learn and complete a task with certain desires or prompts and under certain conditions be it pleasant or unpleasant conditions. The hallmark and greatest potential of humans encompasses the mind and development of mental faculties (and healthy bodies).

These KEYS have been written to empower you and your descendants navigate in this world as masters of your own fate and to avoid falling victims to the misconceptions and other machinations that are keeping millions of people all over the world in bondage and modern-day slavery. Beware of the lurking temptation and enticement of society's 'group-thinking' culture and practices that have robbed many over the centuries of the true understanding and attainment of natural success and further development as a human being.

Over and above all that has been said, these previously held beliefs of success as defined by many famous personalities, public speakers and institutions are rather confusing and contradictory upon critical analysis as it has already shown in the first two KEYS. You may have noticed that there always seem to be something missing in the success seminars, teachings and success models or systems being advertised and sold to the public.

That enabling power to cause the transformation you deeply and sincerely desire is not there and after spending money and time on such rich teachers, gurus or those celebrity speakers often recognised or dubbed as masters of success, you find yourself back to where you started, with little or no improvement in your permanent state of being after that temporary boost or half-baked results have faded out of your life. Such bitter, frustrating and hopeless experiences have made some to believe or wonder if success was meant for others and not for themselves. With such pain and despair, some individuals have conceded to their unfortunate circumstances and concluded or accepted as fact that perhaps only a few have the right to real tangible success in this life and that they have been born under the wrong star and cannot have success in this lifetime of theirs. Well, not so for you.

You are not of that world of hopelessness, and you are definitely not helpless. You have no business subscribing to such ridiculous and laughable circumstances or pseudo-realities. The complete understanding and practice of the principles established within this book is all you need concern yourself with. As long as you follow these KEYS, all is well and it will just be a matter of time and continuous practice. It will make your results known to you and all around you will testify to your results. You cannot fail to be successful by applying yourself to the KEYS laid out in this book.

This book has been put together just for you, to ensure your liberation from a virus that has covertly infiltrated your reality and seeks to sabotage you by intertwining itself with your identity and culture, creating a certain way of life where your development is truncated at each attempt, and every worthy dream aborted before it reaches fruition.

Take a deep breath and continue reading diligently with all eagerness and expectation of becoming a better, more empowered individual through the knowledge you gain. You can do this by remaining calm and consciously or deliberately taking charge of your personal emotions. Control your emotions as the subject of your will rather than letting your emotions control you as though you were the subject to your emotions. Be the king in your life and put in its proper place the usurper, and the subject (your emotions and feelings).

The argument has already been made, and the conclusion drawn that we are in an information age, with an explosion of information from all angles including media and social media outlets, schools, churches and homes on all matters of life including defining success. You may come across those who believe that all those polarised and contradictory or incomplete definitions of success are true in of themselves and that there is no one way to define success, especially with the rapid growth of multiculturalism and diversity. Be very careful of such individuals or such information and the sources from which they came. Never at any point make the mistake of giving them your attention. Avoid them like you would a plague.

While everyone may be entitled to their own personal opinions, these opinions however well-intended they may be or seem does not have the entitlement to rule or take charge of your life. Without a doubt, there is a lot of information on and about success. But the substance, and quality of those informations circulating is what we need to be concerned with and not the large quantities and the large number of support or consensus these untested information and doctrines may have gained.

The time has come for you to put these doctrines or beliefs and information with so much popularity and acceptance through the eternal test. The eternal test is the test to determine the veracity of these popularly accepted information being taught or disseminated as fact and truths. If they are just opinions, then you can be the judge on how to deal with such opinions appropriately. Do not allow such opinions being passed as worthy-knowledge confine your entire life and that of your children to the imaginary prisons created by these opinions of others.

Just as explained in these KEYS, the integrity of a large amount of those informations and definitions or doctrines on the matter of success do not measure up to the test of truth, in that these do not align with facts and reality simultaneously. So the only thing to do is to round up these non-realistic and non-factual success doctrines and just dump them in the dustbin together with the other rubbish since that is exactly where they belong.

Be transformed by the renewing of your mind with fresh, invigorating knowledge that has withstood the test of truth and time. Take this KEY in its totality, leaving nothing behind, because unlike the other information available, the knowledge presented here does not require you to accept it through faith or belief.

The knowledge here before you is uncommon, it is certain, precise and verifiable, putting you in an unshakable, definite state of awareness. With these KEYS, you will be ever ready to recognise and make full use opportunities wherever they may present themselves. Therefore, you do not require faith in the presence of such definite, unshakable knowledge. Faith or belief is not required in the presence of true knowledge because faith or belief is defined as having complete trust and confidence or strong convictions in the presumed existence of something or someone you cannot prove empirically or have no concrete, direct knowledge on. This is the exact opposite when dealing with true knowledge. For example, if a police officer asked you about the ownership of the car in your possession, which was your property, your own car, you would not reply "I have faith this car is mine officer", or you would be arrested on the spot on the charge of auto theft until all doubts are cleared. This example is one of the countless ways to show that definite knowledge totally eradicates and negates the need for faith or belief.

Now the confusion becomes so clear and understandable why many cannot achieve 'success' even after spending so much money, time and dedication chasing success gurus and powerful motivational speakers. Have you ever critically considered why many individuals after achieving their goals and objectives of leaving behind poverty and becoming rich will give television interviews, write in books, blogs or on social media pages they no longer consider success to be about large sums of currency or money?

In the media today, we see disturbing and predictable trends with many so called successful individuals, super rich individuals, Hollywood super-stars and business tycoons becoming suicidal, suffering with drug addiction and alcohol abuse among other destructive behaviours. Have you considered why a lot of successful people after choosing to go through hell and many unthinkable sacrifices for fame and money which they consider 'success', will become suicidal, suffer with drug addiction and alcohol abuse among other destructive behaviours?

More often than not, the major reason in most cases is the fact that these individuals often labelled stars and successful personalities were with great dedication and determination, climbing the ladder of success, only to get to the top of that supposed success ladder and realise that they had all this time been climbing up a mislabelled ladder. What a shock.

There is only one way to become a successful being and only one way to achieve this, as stated earlier in the success definition above. All else is nothing but the expression of opinions, feelings and wishes surrounding the all-important topic of being successful. So for your own benefit, do not get mis-educated or misguided and confused over the matter that has now been settled and laid bare before you.

As my dearly beloved brother often said to me in conversations about dreams, "see success as a shadow…". This, in fact, is a great analogy that I will now share with you. He further explains that "each one of us have our own shadow and you do not in your right mind chase after your shadow, unless you are a little child playing or having fun as kids often do, just like what we used to back in the days when we were kids, trying to jump onto our own shadows and so on, for laughs. Just as each individual has their own shadow, the same goes for success, and so the potential to become successful is there, for every individual. In the right light with the right positioning, you will cast a perfect, complete shadow and this shadow will follow you wherever you go, just as success will be your testimony once you possess that right, empowering knowledge of liberation". This is a lesson on success I have never, and will never forget.

You can never see your shadow in the absence of light. All you need to do to disprove this is to stand in the middle of your room with no lights entering that room, and turn your lights off, then try to locate your shadow. It cannot be done either naturally or supernaturally. In life, this stage of the absence of light, or lack of illumination signifies a state of ignorance, lack of knowledge and wisdom. This state of naivety is not a good place to be in and there is nothing cute or adorable about being naïve, because naivety just means lacking wisdom, lacking right judgement and lacking critical knowledge and there is nothing adorable about a dumb, ignorant individual who is said to be naïve (lacking wisdom or right judgment).

I still have not found to this day the reason many think it is sweet and adorable to be naïve (lacking wisdom or right judgment) and equate this to being pure or innocent. Beware of such people. You can be the purest human in existence and still be an intelligent and successful person and maintain your integrity and innocence and all other great virtues. Be careful of those who would attempt or work to keep you ignorant, to keep you in the dark abysmal place of ignorance and away from the true knowledge of yourself and of the world in which you live. Such individuals have just declared to you openly but quietly that they are your sworn, natural enemies and an enemy has no good and noble plans for you now or in the future.

So do not love your enemies or you will perish in your love for them.

If loving your enemy was the right thing and the good thing to do, the Jewish or Christian God or Yahweh claimed to be the embodiment of all Goodness, would have set the greatest example to love his enemy which is said to be Satan. Yet the All-loving God hates this arch-enemy with a passion and will burn that devil in eternal fire together with some sinners and patronisers of Satan the arch-enemy. At least if you do not want to learn from me, learn from the God/Yahweh that is taught or preached in the Bible or Torah or Quran just this once.

Your enemy will never empower you or do good to you under any circumstance. So beware and keep your head straight, and in the right place. Stop being a victim and stop being the happy, hopeful, peace-loving and noble slave that your society produces. Who sold you the lie that there was anything happy, hopeful, peace-loving and noble about being an oppressed victim or slave? There is nothing happy, hopeful, peace-loving and noble about being a slave or victim or struggler/hustler and there is no secret reward prepared for you in the sky or in any place called paradise.

Know that you can never see your shadow in a dark room until you turn on the lights or open the windows and doors to let in sunlight. Only then can your body cast a shadow. The light entering is the entrance of knowledge of self, and the self-awareness of the individual brings about the success of that individual through mental transformation or the washing of the mind if you will (that is freeing your mind from all the pollution and illusions keeping it bound under its spell). This analogy puts the explanation of success in a much more practical way for all to see, understand and relate to. And like a shadow, success will follow naturally, once you can take charge of your mind and develop your mental faculties. You can only be successful by being yourself and not by being anyone else or imitating another individual you admire.

This success as an individual we are referring to is timeless and holistic;It is far from making a few profits on your financial investments. All these material things classed as success is but secondary, or peripheral matters in the attainment of the holistic, natural success that has been unveiled here in this book. You can think of this 'Success' as the creator or way-maker preceding all other accomplishments that are noteworthy. It is an amazing feat to accomplish in its own right and it all starts with you being and acting in your right mind and right person or identity.

Once that success is realised or completely manifested in you, you will have a new perspective on life itself. You will realise that all things in your life are falling into their right and proper place, and all things will become new. You will have new desires and refined thoughts in most cases among many other positive self-empowering changes, abilities, and wonderful experiences you never imagined before. Your life at that point can only be described as sweet, or for some, the good life. You can say you have become a new person at this point. You can then congratulate and celebrate yourself.

You will have a new self-appreciation and self-esteem, your development and everything relating to you will be in wonderful harmony and perfect synchrony. You will know peace and fulfilment like never before and your understanding, appreciation and love for life, family, and relationships will be at an all-time high. From that point on is when the real work that counts the most in your life begins. That is why I stated earlier that the attainment of success has defined parameters that must be respected. It is not a mere continuous journey or cycle. At best, it can be described as a difficult journey more so than a long journey.

2.4 Seeking The Right Knowledge

In seeking the right knowledge to apply, we will do well to make a mental note and not forget that words (sound or voice) play a very important role not only in society but also in the mental arena or otherwise referred to as the spiritual world by some.

In the science of communication alone, words can play a massive role, and there is a reason for that, as I alluded to previously. A short test verifying this is the erection based on a mere sound or words spoken into the ears of a male individual. All that was needed was a word or two, a sound, and the whole male biochemistry gets on fire with passion and desire. This is the magic of sound. This is a kind of mystery, but the good news is that this mystery is an understandable mystery.

A lot of males can definitely attest to this truth in case you were not aware of it. Another reason for being mindful of the role words or sounds have to play is the fact that words including intonation seem to evoke all kinds of emotions and desires, regardless of the present reality, making false communication and propaganda a powerful but dangerous tool in the possession and exploitation of the wicked and inhuman.

If you lack imagination, then you eventually cease to be creative. Once you cease to create, you cannot prepare adequately for the future. This lack of preparation for the future causes you to remain stagnant and thus you cease to grow at all levels. And once you have ceased from growth, you will soon dwindle or regress. Keep dwindling, keep regressing, and you will soon fade out of existence, giving up your very own life and the life of your descendants to come after you. At this final stage, you have become obsolete and thus your existence itself becomes inconsequential.

Aside from losing respect and recognition from any other groups of people or communities, you will be considered and treated by all others as trash and as the filth of the earth. You lose everything vital that is needed and necessary for a fruitful and independent life. Everything worthwhile will be out of reach for you and the physical resources necessary for your sustenance will become a scarce commodity, constantly eluding you. All these things show a good use and command of one's imagination and as any human with a vivid, active imagination will admit, the sky which is a limit for most, is just the beginning once the human imagination is fully engaged.

The only way to harness such great potential power in words and intonation is only through the proper understanding and usage of the words and intonations. Learning to use your imagination is key to unveiling all the potential power stored in words and other forms of knowledge acquisition processes, including reading. Therefore, the necessity of learning to use one's own imagination is a very important feat or achievement and even more so when combined with the right sounds or words.

For example, you may use words to express how you feel about something but you can agree that you use your imaginations to begin or generate and maintain that moment of pleasure, anger or happiness that has just been evoked through the meditation and mental reflection on those spoken words. That is your creative imagination at work, creating a scene that has just been spoken about in a few words or sentences.

Take this example you can easily relate to, regardless of your current social status or condition. You are told by words or through writing that you have a sum of two and a half million British pound sterling (£2.5M) deposited at a nearby hotel in your name awaiting your collection and a labelled access key to that room is immediately presented to you. These words or messages you have just heard or read invariably create a certain imagination or mental and emotional state within your brain and entire being. This imagination invokes a certain euphoria or bliss and excitement even though you may not have received in your possession the physical equivalent of those listed items and promises for which you are so excited. In that moment, if you were feeling down, you would for an instant be uplifted emotionally.

You may even go to the extent of planning ahead of time, what you will do with all that money, where you would go, which girl or boy you would date or try to date, which countries you would like to visit and so on.

Conversely, if you had received a bad news instead, for example, news of the death of a close relation or a close acquaintance, your heart would most likely skip a beat, and you would panic as sorrow wells up within you. You will be overwhelmed with fear, disbelief, and pain. You would respond to this news not only mentally but also physiologically, as you begin to pant heavily, as though you had just completed a 20km marathon in less than 2minutes. You would sweat even if it was the coldest day of winter as you stood in the same spot without having to move a muscle. That is the power of imagination and you can use that to your advantage as directed here in this book, carefully following the established KEYS and the volumes of writings to follow.

We all know that many leaders have supposedly been well educated on how to use the machinery of civilisation to rule over their countries and other national and international organisations. They may have gained these forms of education from parts of Asia, Western Europe, or the USA. Yet we observe through eyewitness accounts, and on the various media platforms that the current leadership in many countries are ill-fitted to direct the affairs of humanity in their respective nations and have proven time and time again their inability to sustain or even attempt to advance civilisation in their region.

However, they seem very effective at making television appearances and sending empty, deceitful warnings and sweet-sounding but empty promises before, during, and after political elections. What could be going on here? Is it a case of amnesia, lack of constructive thinking, absolute incompetency, corrupted minds entrusted with power, or a secret form of a diabolically orchestrated plan to serve the ends of a selected few backing these international catastrophes in the shadows? Do not be phased even though the right answer here is all the above.

Day in day out, we are faced with a very sad reality and unimaginable crisis on an individual level and a global level, on this planet we call home. It is very hard and unpleasant to admit this reality but the fact remains with us to date that there is a big lack of pure, authentic and brave, selfless leaders in the fields of politics, economics, armed forces and the military, religious or otherwise. That is why we are where we are today and a bigger part of this problem, interestingly rests on the shoulders of every citizen, rich or poor, male or female.

In an age of so-called explosion of knowledge, it is clear that most men and most women of today with all their education and years of experiences which they proudly boast of has been and still is insufficient to successfully manage and direct the process and progress of human development and civilisation. The simple process of just maintaining our present civilisation in peace and with respect for one another alone has now become supremely complex and demands incalculably subtle powers in ensuring such maintenance is achieved.

Such skill and ability for the mere preservation and maintenance of our current world to avoid running the world into chaos, terrorism and unending wars is so lacking among current leadership pools to where the current governments and their leaderships throughout the world are failing miserably with their own targets and ability to dialogue and get some decent results that doesn't involve obfuscation and white lies (lies that are supposed to be good for its hearers, probably following this 'white' prefix rule, society might argue that a 'white'-terrorist is good for the terrorised individuals if am not mistaken).

In a broken society, a failed international consensus, the magic of prefixing 'white' to something as bad as a lie, for example, suddenly makes the 'lie' something better, something right, and worthy of acceptance by people and society. Does it not? That is for you to answer and reflect on.

At this point it is safe and correctly so to conclude that the world at large is now crying for a new breed of saviours, ones who will bring back order, restore dignity and sanity to humanity and allow for the flourishing of the entire human family or species. It appears humans are their own worst enemies and no other species need become the enemy of humans, for they simultaneously occupy that role of being human while hating themselves.

I deliberately chose this wording to say humans are acting as themselves and not being themselves because once you know yourself, accept who you are meant to be and become yourself, you will love yourself and cease from being an enemy and a hater to yourself and to your own kind and family. It is that simple. You need not waste time like others pretending to be human when you can become one and live as one who is human. You pretend without a cause, and this is only futility of futilities; it is vanity of vanities. When will you wake up from this meaninglessness dear one?

As mentioned earlier, a big part of the reason for this sad reality in this current world is the root-ignorance of the very origins and principles of humanity and the origin and gradual development of human culture and civilisation. Such information has been craftily distorted by ruthless conspiracies and specific groups serving as covert agents through infiltrations, subversions, terrorisms and so on, educating the masses wrongfully, acting as experts misguiding foreign governments and using the media as an effective too and medium for the spread of their well-written agendas, while building highly efficient machines by combining media, education systems, military, economic, scientific, religious and political systems for global domination and a new world order under their leadership.

And until that is addressed, and remedied, there will be no solution to the rapid spreading of global terrorism, slavery, colonialism, imperialism, armed conflicts and world wars, corruptions and other engineered viruses and atrocities plaguing the nations of the world today. Talk about prayer and fasting, peace, love, hope, or faith and these things will lead you only to one place you fear the most, a place called an early grave, where you die before the maturity of your natural time of death. Things have already been set in motion but for what it is worth, it means you have absolutely nothing to lose and much to gain by taking a decisive and bold action against the current.

No amount of debate, labour strikes or protests, referendums or voting, democratic and non-democratic elections can solve such a monstrous system with these terrifying capabilities. Thankfully, the solution has already been fully outlined, for the liberation of the nations.

The problem we face is the Complex-Never-Changing-Lock and before you right now is the Almighty-Never-Changing-Key that negates and eradicates completely the current problem. The strict adherence and continuous practice of the concepts and principles on success and being a successful human or individual as presented in this book is the sure remedy and a way to right the wrongs and exterminate the problems of our world we live in now regardless of which part of the world you may live in.

No man is an island. This is why: Their problems yesterday became your problems today and your problems today if unchecked and resolved will become our problems tomorrow. With one voice we will not have that. You cannot be so poor or so rich to a point where you become immune to the erratic global spreading of human problems. This is because nature abhors vacuum and that is why humanity with all its problems will eventually catch up to you wherever you may be, whether you stay in the most secure safe house, a remote village off-grid, or in the backside of a hippo. There is no hiding place and nowhere is safe until it is over. Some problems cannot just go away by wishing and praying them away, except they be dealt with in all earnestness and seriousness.

Concluding statement: Free your mind, Free yourself.

KEY 3: YOUR MIND, YOUR LIFE

"All the power you would need comes from within
and thus all you need is within, under your control."

Fidelis Bassuah (Fidpal)

3.0 Unveiling Your True Potential

The truth of the matter is that no one on this planet even knows the limits of your true greatness or potential. Usually, we either place limits on ourselves or our close relations or society or organisation places limits on us and this is not a true reflection of the limits to our abilities or capabilities. The current consensus in academia on the major subjects that works together to give us a better understanding of ourselves as humans can generally be divided into two parts. These are science (including human anatomy and physiology, medicine, psychology, chemistry and all other relevant subsets) and philosophy. Both subjects point to one thing about humans, that we have infinite potential and we are yet to seek effective ways for harnessing such great human potential.

Looking at this on the grand scheme of things, the internet for example has always been here on this planet, the airplane has always been here with humanity, x-ray and the Magnetic Resonance Imaging (MRI) and artificial intelligence have all been with us and it took some time for these inventions and developments which were once visions and imaginations or ideas and dreams of others to be transmuted or translated into their physical equivalence.

An example is the strange story of Guglielmo Marconi. He was a scientist who was reported to be mentally deranged by his fellow friends and scientists and kept in an asylum for further observation after he told his friend of his idea of producing wireless communications in the late 1890s. This scientist never gave up and after his release from the asylum (psychiatric hospital), he carried on with his scientific dream of attempting to make some wireless equipment for radio communication. He later became very famous in his time for being the one who invented the first system of radio communication via experiments in wireless telegraphy and began the revolutionary wave of wireless communication in the Western world. After such astonishing efforts, they awarded him the Nobel Prize for Physics in 1909.

From space travel to time travel, to human rockets, there are much greater things for us to invent, to develop and enjoy if only we would allow ourselves to think these wonders into our physical world.

All lives can be counted but after all has been said and done, not all counted lives are equal. Not that any one life is superior to the other but the gradual unfolding and outworking of a life gives the distinguishing character to that life. And the unfolding and potentials in each life is unique and hence no two people are ever the same, because Nature is particular, very amazing and never runs out of ideas. That is why even identical twins have different fingerprints among many other distinct features, though they may both be formed from a single zygote within the womb of the mother. So while all may be created equal, all lives are not identical and thus all lives are not equal.

You are unique and different so be proud of yourself and embrace who you are. And so make your life count for the better. Plan for your life. You cannot live life especially in these times without a plan or with no form of planning. Half a plan is better than no plan at all. Either you plan for your life or someone else will plan it directly or indirectly for you.

So what is it going to be for you? Get serious, but always remember to laugh a little as often as you can for laughter does good to your heart, soul and body, and it is the medicine you cannot buy at the pharmacy or drug store. Both your physical and mental wellbeing requires periodic laughter. So get smart, learn, study well and be happy while you are at it. Don't be lazy in learning and developing yourself.

It is definitely possible that something unique will happen even as you read this material. You may immediately identify with or connect with some or all of the things you are reading here and it's because you already know these things or at least possess within you some elements or parts of these KEYS. Here, you can say I am just here to confirm and re-echo certain truths to you, to bridge the gap between those aspects of truths that will resonate within you, connecting the dots to the attainment of the physical manifestations in the outside world where you now live. This is actually a different form of inspiration, not the usual 'feel good' inspiration that produces an emotional euphoria and temporary happiness. This kind of inspiration here is the uncommon art of empowering you to make that leap from where you are into a new and better life you envision or desire.

For some, becoming a successful individual will be completely achieved in a shorter time, requiring less self-discipline and self-sacrifices of lesser intensity. But for others, the achievement of this holistic success as an individual will require longer for the full manifestation of the right results. This may involve requiring more effort and more self-discipline and conscientiously reading the

KEYS, bit by bit daily, continuously without missing a day, and repeating this until you have fully read the entire KEYS in this publication for at least 7 consecutive times. Ideally, try to read this entire publication at least 7 times (and in multiples of 7-eg: 7 or 14, or 21 times) within six months and repeat this as long as necessary until the expected results manifest in your life.

Even at this stage you still need to continue feeding your mind on these KEYS among other reference materials mentioned if possible, to ensure that you cease all possibilities of reverting to the old self, old destructive habits or falling back to the lower plane. As you may have heard, old habits die hard but what they didn't tell you is that bad habits die the hardest. The difference in the time and effort needed to achieve such a holistic success is mainly due to individual differences, mental state prior to commencement of reading the KEYS, your environment will power and growth capabilities. If it seems to take longer than you expected, then you perhaps need to readjust yourself, re-test yourself, and let things fall in their right place.

Do your best and have the right desire, and you will have started your journey to success the right way. Nature will aid you in such a noble, divine quest as you embark on this endeavour so do not lose hope or feel you need to know everything and how everything will turn out before you begin. Just begin and you will be given the power to do that which must be done, one step at a time, one leap after another till you leave your current plane of existence onto the higher, heavenly plane. You have more potential stored in you to empower you than you can imagine.

Try not to fall into a bad habit of doing the same thing over and over and expecting a different result, because that will never end well for you. Do not expect the mental state or way of thinking that has brought you some problems to be the same mental state you rely on to solve those problems. The best way is to look at those old, persisting problems in a new light, with a newly developed mental state. It is time for an upgrade, for a mental upgrade. Renew your mind and thinking, and you would have renewed your personality. Once that activation of your previously dormant inner self and inner abilities has occurred, then your success story is already in motion and cannot be stopped at this point.

Being successful as a human being is more of a dynamic, self-sustaining foundation than anything else. For you the reader, the right focus becomes the attainment of the right foundation in life as opposed to the chasing of some ideals in the near or distant future in a life-long journey. You may not even have that long a time as you thought you did.

Even if you had a lot of time, what worth is there in it for you to chase some ideals, or material possessions and properties while neglecting the essence and value of the very wonderful gift of life you now possess? That is why it is so important to dedicate time and effort to the art of self-discovery. And if you could know yourself well, you would have the inner ability to intelligently manage your emotions and this alone can dramatically improve your life beyond expectation as this means you will be better positioned to succeed in life.

Once you have become yourself again, you will shed away all unnecessary weights and know what works for you and what does not work for you. Your time management will be effective and your actions will be more efficient in getting the right results timely.

You are the major key to your better future, and there is no other way around it. No one can make you successful or set you free but yourself. Freedom can never be given. Freedom is always obtained by taking. No human or nation in the last 10,000 years of recorded history and beyond ever received freedom.

Freedom has always and will always be something that has to be taken and protected. We now have to fight for freedom and fight or be ever ready to defend the freedom we have obtained by fighting to keep it whenever the threat to our freedom arises, because we are no longer living on this planet alone. We are not alone. The one who takes his or her freedom is the one who becomes free. In that same way, the nation that takes its freedom is the same nation that becomes free.

You cannot negotiate or beg for or buy your freedom. That is just a concept portrayed in a TV drama series or in a comedy show to entertain people as they laugh to the unrealistic and often idiotic concept of a bond servant or prisoner of war negotiating their freedom with their captors or engaging an usurper in a democratic dialogue to restore the stolen throne and power to the legitimate King or Queen and rightful rulers. The one who becomes free is not the one who demands or begs or debates about the prospect of being free.

The best contribution others can give you or make available to you if they desire to do so is present you with the technical knowhow or the principles which you must then take upon yourself and follow methodically with all the willpower available to you to take your freedom or make that transformation you desire. This has always been the only way to freedom, and this will continue to be the case long after you leave this physical world. So it is better to drop the egotism and stubbornness, and instead work to be the best we can through determination, self-assertion and the application of the right knowledge.

By following these important principles, this world of humans in which we live can be a better, more accommodating one with plenty of resources available to all. Then there will be no more room for unhealthy, immoral, unnecessary and artificially created international policies of fierce competitions, false pretences and deceitful ideologies which are all rooted in oppression and miseducation, hatred and terrorism and all the other hallmarks of the current world we now have to deal with. Either we wake up and correct the wrongs of this world before everything is corrupted and destroyed beyond the point of corruption, or we find a new planet and start over again.

The best and most pragmatic solution is always to choose an easier, more plausible and effective solution. Here, that is to change the current world we have, to make it a liveable place, a better place for not only ourselves but for the entire human population and for the generations to come. We owe at least that much to the great ones that came before us, and those that are to come after us even if we decide we have no interest in helping those around. This is a far better way forward, and a much more reasonable solution to the national and international problems we face than the other option of flying into space in search of a new habitable planet.

If we cannot fix this mess, chances are we cannot do so well on an even better and more resourceful planet than this one we call earth. As per simple logic, even if we found another similar or parallel earth we could move and live happily, we would take the same ailments and problems to the new planet and in the long run it will not end well.

As above, so below, as within, so beyond and there is no escaping this law that governs reality. So we have but one choice, one solution, one way to aim for, and that is to become successful in this life for ourselves and our loved ones and the entire nations of humans on this plane we call earth.

3.1 The Mind And Life

As you continue reading, it is important to make a mental note of this wise statement of fact made by Dr. Ray Hagins, that "great minds discuss ideas, average minds discuss events, and small minds discuss people". Sincerely categorise yourself accordingly to which of the above Minds you possess and make the adjustments and transitions necessary. Dr. Ray Hagins is a famous American Spiritual Leader and teacher. He is also a renowned clinician, therapist, a musician, and a pilot.

These are well researched, detailed accounts presented here in the most succinct and pragmatic format for effective delivery and easy understanding, without the addition of the usual jargons and extra opinions and empty philosophies. I do this to save you the reader precious time. After you have attained that real and holistic success, you can chase after theories and philosophies all you want till your heart is content if that is what you will to do.

The matter of Mind and Life is very important and you as a reader may need to have a critical conversation with yourself and ask yourself a question or two, even before we get down to the details of this matter of Mind and Life. One of the vital questions you may need to consider is this: are you alive or are you existing? Again, are you definitely alive or definitely existing? These two words are not the same and definitely have different implications depending on which category you fall in or put yourself into. To exist does not mean to be alive, and there is a big difference in the two states of being in understanding the human world. The state of being 'Alive' demands your activeness, production, growth and participation continuously, whereas the state of 'Existence' in fact requires nothing of such sort from you. Thus, it is essential you assess and categorise yourself accordingly. Make a stand and this KEY can help you do exactly that. If you desire to move from one class to another, from your current plane to a higher plane, this KEY will provide you with the know-how and principles through which you can be empowered to make that quantum leap into the group you belong or wish to identify with and your developed will power is an integral part of the process.

There is a big difference in thinking and presuming that you are thinking. Many people all over the world have fallen for the same trap of something I shall call 'Imagined Thinking'. I have carefully chosen the term 'imagined-thinking' for the sake of simplicity and ease of communication. This terminology is also self-explanatory. This condition I have just named is so pervasive, with sufferers in every known country, existing in all levels of society, yet this case or psychosis as is the proper and existing psychiatric and medical terminology in psychology and medicine is rarely ever talked about in society.

Unfortunately, many unsuspecting and innocent individuals have fallen victims to such psychological conditions which can and have actually been artificially engineered within societies by our fellow men and their organisations (both known and unknown societies or organisations) to gain socio-economical power and control over certain groups and classes of people.

The effect of such psychosis is countless and sometimes unpredictable in the lives of individuals both affected and unaffected individuals who may live side by side and interact with one another daily. Some devastating effects of this psychosis we talk about is the unexplained chaos in lives and communities that seem to have no end, the continuous and common issues divorces, broken marriages, broken homes and the destruction of families and relationships.

It is a fact that these occurrences have become so frequent and common in this century and in our time that these things have now been taken for granted and accepted as a common part of life and society. You may know or have noticed a neighbour or some colleagues at school or work or at your social club who may have fallen victims to such unfortunate occurrences and you may think to yourself that it is well with you because this does not affect you personally or directly and thus you have no part in this. This is not entirely true because as they say, no man is an island, and no woman is an island and you cannot live in isolation from all societies forever, that defeats the purpose of communal living, and communal instincts of a human being which you are. For how long would you be willing to deny yourself the expressions of love, relationship, and communion with fellow humans?

If you choose to ignore someone in need, it will be your turn to be in need the next time, and eventually you too will have no one to concern themselves with you, with your suffering or troubles, for they too will say it is your personal problem so you deal with it. With such a crucial and devastating phenomenon destroying lives and nations, why is there no formal and systematic structures and systems in place to combat this and why is the media or experts and academia not covering such topics or putting it at the forefront of their activities to educate the masses, that is the people they are already disseminating news and information to? Are they waiting to act at the time when people fight unceasingly in their numbers for their right to be allowed to rape, sell drugs, murder and commit serial murders among other degeneracies just because they have a strong inclination to do so?

It is a sad story because people who may find themselves trapped in such conditions are often not aware of it or the consequences during their entire lifetime, probably because of high unending volumes of pressure, responsibilities and duties, fierce competition and the many distractions that have become a normal part of every day 'city' life (called modern-lifestyle) for many men and women, whether they be in formal education, jobs or anywhere else.

You can search the dictionary or medical definition for the word psychosis to have a better understanding of the problem being discussed here. Then you can calmly sit down and have a simple, yet deep assessment of your life and what you see and deal with around you, and see if anything including your inner beliefs, faith, thoughts or practice is inconsistent with external and physical realities around you. The aim of this exercise is not to make you feel sad, or condemn yourself but this is a special lifetime opportunity for you to get back on your feet and be the best you you can ever be, because that greatness is in you too and your coming into this world was never an accident.

In hindsight, one can see that it is not that easy, to realise that you are not running on your own original thoughts but that you are running on an artificially and subliminally engineered mental program or mindset you were exposed to and subjected to, perhaps during the earlier stages of your lifetime.

In such a case, all you will know and all you will be proud of and protect is that which you were taught, and that which you know. So it is expected that you will automatically trigger a 'learned' reaction and quick response in defence of what you know all your life once you get any new message or hear something new that is not in your circle of awareness and something not in your circle of knowledge. You may even feel that your personality and culture is being attacked by the incoming new information you are not aware of and you may have all kinds of emotions and anger and fear welling up in you.

But try your best to calm yourself down, take slow deep breaths and if necessary, listen to that new information without overreacting or being too overwhelmed by what you read, see or hear because it is all part of the process of mental development. It is expected, and so stay calm and free yourself. Your time of favour and liberation has come. And don't forget to smile too.

Reading this alone can help individuals who are ready to make that leap out of the subliminal control to break open and escape that seal or spell that was cast over you and causing you to be in that condition you are in. While many may not recognise they suffer from this condition, there are some who end up realising the condition after a big shock, or a near death experience or other life threatening, agonising and regrettable experiences. That you are not aware of something does not mean that the thing you do not know ceases to exist. It however means you will be ignorant of the modus operandi of that thing or condition you know nothing about and you will be ignorant to its effect on you if any at all.

As you have realized earlier, the condition I referred to as 'Imagined Thinking', again is a condition where the individual does not think and yet is seriously and confidently convinced and believe that she or he is thinking, is well informed and well educated, when all they are doing, is in fact following a pre-installed synthetic program and multiple auto-suggestions that has been successfully deposited in their subconscious and conscious mind.

Food for thought

1. Is it possible to be in a prison and not know that you are in a prison?

2. Is it possible to give birth and raise children in a (well-resourced) prison, with these children growing up into adulthood without ever knowing they have been living in a prison complex all their life?

The answer to both of the above questions is a resounding Yes. If you have not seen the movie called The Truman Show, I would like to recommend that you watch this movie in your spare time. Although it is an old movie that was released in 1998 it is worth watching. Watch the entire movie and you will not regret a minute of it once the movie is over. This can add to your understanding why the answers for both questions above is yes.

3.2 Tapping Into Untapped Power

Before you continue reading, let us go over some fundamental yet often missed facts about humans. Below are some interesting scientific facts in the world of neuroscience that will cause you to pause and wonder or marvel at your own inherent abilities, the super powers lying dormant in you that no one made time to explicitly tell you so you could understand. Your brain power is your natural resource. This is a personal resource of which you can have no control or 100%, total control over, should you desire it.

Did you know that the average human brain processes about 400 billion (400,000,000,000) bits of information per second? Did you also know that the human brain is the most complex tissue scientists have studied to date in the entire universe?

However, of the 400 billion bits of information processed per second by the brain, humans are usually only conscious of about 2000 bits of the processed information out of the 400 billion bits of information processed within the human brain per second. Such huge figures may sound impressive but the truth of the matter is that these 400 billion bits of information that can be processed per second by the human brain is nowhere near the full capacity or limit of the amount of bits of information that can be processed by a single human brain. Such is the power of your own personal brain.

This will come as no shock once you know that the average human uses only about 5%-7% of their entire brain capacity, for the entirety of their human lifetime. This means throughout their entire life span, humans, including yourself only end up using roughly about only 5% or probably 10% (if you try hard enough) of their own brain capacity.

I wonder why the large conservation of brain power. For what purpose is this extreme conservation of brain power one may ask? Perhaps someday someone can let us in on the secret why humans are using the smallest capacity of their brain power their entire life, year after year, generation after generation at the risk of their own peril.

With this, I can only conclude that you have much greater potential than you might imagine, and do not doubt me. After all you are only using less than 10% of your brain capacity, even for those smart individuals seen as geniuses are tapping into only somewhere about 15% of their brain capacities at most for all the wonders they seem to do, so what do you really know about yourself? Just accept the reality. You can do better, do much more than you are doing now. So what you call your best now is really not your best.

That which you call your best now is the best you can do at your lowest capacity and does not take into account the best you can do at your full potential. You can do better only when you become self-aware and before you finish reading this book, you would have identified the right path to unlocking your great potential that has been lying dormant deep within YOU.

Your thoughts and thinking rightly activated and channelled will cause a transformation in your way of life and this life transformation will be so influential that it will cause the creation of a new habit, a new personality and cause your surroundings and environment to change and adjust to the new you. That is what you can call an 'Awakening' as your environment responds to your innermost will while your experience and appreciation for nature is magnified.

Concluding statement: Free your mind, Free yourself.

KEY 4: UNDERSTANDING THE MONOPOLISATION AND MONETISATION OF GOD

"Lies have many variations but truth has none. As a matter of fact, the speaker of truth has no friends."

Christina Konadu (CK)

4.0 Why Is Freethinking A Forbidden Fruit

So why do you think the church should ban or discourage implicitly or explicitly its congregation, the so-called believer, from being open-minded or from being free thinkers? Doesn't the God(s) of the churches and other religions want the believers to be sound minded and authentic individuals? The lack of agreement among believers of the same faith on the core beliefs of their faith, their holy scriptures and religious practices. Is church really all about what we traditionally think church is about seeking God's will and salvation, or is church an exalted business model?

Do you know that churches and church-related activities in the United States of America (USA) contributes more to the national economy of the USA than the top ten American technology companies? According to a report by DW television network in Germany, the church in Germany is worth 345 billion euros as of 2017. This is just a summary of the worth of the Germany-based churches within Germany, and these churches are all supposed to be non-government and not-for-profit organisations.

Note to reader: While it is not necessarily good or bad for any individual to join a religion of any kind, and carry out their cultural practices, the following presentation is a collection of historical facts and case studies from past and current affairs. These things are happening around us and thus are not a debatable topic. It is only a matter of observation.

Did you know that there are over four thousand two hundred (4,200) different religions on this planet? Out of these four thousand two hundred (4,200) different religions, leading the list is the Christian religion or as it is commonly known, Christianity. Now within Christianity alone, there are over thirty thousand (30,000) different sects with diverse beliefs and doctrines all under Christianity.

Members of those 30,000 or more sects within Christianity all live their lives and carry themselves differently according to their line of belief or the branch or sect of Christianity they have adopted. So, for example, you could have five Christian friends and all five of them would hold slightly different doctrines and different fundamental beliefs in relation to god, the identity of god and what Christianity is or means to them and their particular faith or sect they follow within Christianity.

Did you ever wonder why there are so many variations on the exact, same subject and identity? All the different sects under Christianity alone have different holy books, holy bibles or scriptures and other literature that claims exclusivity to hold the truth and being the right way. Fortunately or unfortunately for some, this is also the case in all the other mainstream religions worldwide.

Did you also know that the church since its beginning as far back as some 2000 years ago from the dawn of the Roman empire till the 20th century as we speak, has always and still opposes and discourages individuals from being rational, from being open-minded or engaging in freethinking? The church again from its creation, throughout its history to date, does all it can in its practices and legislations to shut down nonconformists, enlightened or independent thinkers.

The fact of the matter is that, in every nation where the church has been established, the church has engaged in the same underhanded practices using different names and using semantics to confuse and confine the minds of the masses and innocent individuals seeking spirituality and ways of enlightenment. This is deplorable and unacceptable for the churches of today, especially when this systemically corrupt organisations of commerce called churches or temples internationally prey on the individuals and families in the darkest hours and most vulnerable moments of their lives.

Most of us have been past victims of this devilish, soulless scheme and we speak not from a philosophical or hearsay account but from life experiences and back these up with living tangible proofs.

This wonderful act of independent, rational, freethinking is actually known as the crime of heresy in religion and according to the Ecclesiastical laws and church doctrines. This freethinking or heresy according to the church is the greatest sin and a crime against the church and is punishable by death and eternal damnation of your soul after your sanctioned execution.

After condemnation for being a freethinker according to the church, you are executed. Yes, you are executed by the church like a criminal and the church teaches that just as you faced a death penalty in your physical body, your spirit once it leaves your body will be further condemned in a place called hell (hell fire or hades). This hell or hades is said to be a place of despair, where those who are unfortunate enough to end up there will suffer for eternity agonising pain, with gnashing of teeth in the heat of an unquenchable fire.

With all the science and glaring facts to the contrary, reality in modern society has somehow been morphed systematically into something so bizarre, so esoteric and mysterious in the eyes and minds of many people to where it has now become almost impossible to become enlightened on the true state of reality and the unfavourable reality that has been pulled over the natural reality of this world. The response you will often get for lifting up one from the prison they do not realise they are in will be that of mockery or hostility.

In such a lost society with fear, conspiracies and deception or politricks (political trickery) as the order of the day, those evil and corrupt individuals or officials will be highly rewarded financially and with promotions while those honest, authentic and pure of heart individuals or officials will be oppressed, framed, deceived, enslaved and made to face sanctions and discrimination and injustice daily. Perhaps this is the reason very few people are honest and direct in the world.

The cost of being an authentic, honest civil service and a person with principles is too high and most would rather choose the other path to avoid all these hassles and persecution. Perhaps examples of these artificial realities people are now living under can be seen in concepts like the collective and social acceptance of allowing a lie to get a moral pass if it is qualified with the colour 'white'. Therefore, every white lie according to our modern society is considered not considered a lie.

You can see that someone is really out to extinguish the existence of truth, reality and nobility at all cause, by any means necessary and that is no light matter. Truth and reality in which we all live is our home and now that this planet we live on is under attack from within, the question is: What do you plan to do about this terrible, diabolic warfare being waged against the fabric or foundation of your reality and nature?

There is in our modern societies many other similar common sayings that may have many forms depending on the continent or nation in which you live. They all have one thing in common, to make you feel that telling a lie is all right and that the truth is something that can be overlooked for as long as is possible.

I give a few examples below for your perusal and if you are in the habit of using any of them, perhaps reconsider not using them, to help make human society a better place to live in. White lies won't hurt anyone; a white lie now and then does no harm; White lie is better than an outright lie; Little white lies here and there is human nature; everyone does that occasionally.

There are endless quotes glamorising, supporting, downplaying or describing white lies and its bizarre relationship to human nature and society. This form of brainwashing on a global scale will sensitise societies to spreading and accepting lies as the norm and simultaneously producing in the reverse deep-seated rejection or disdain for truth and anything connected to the truth. By constantly feeding on lies, you will accept and see that "White lies keep social dignity intact and are far more prevalent than most people realise.

Several studies have found that an average person is lied to from 10 to 200 times a day - mostly just to keep a conversation going, to avoid conflict, or to establish a connection with someone". "Lying is a cooperative act. Think about it. A lie has no power whatsoever by its mere utterance. Its power emerges when someone else agrees to believe the lie."

These quotes from Pamela Meyer (as portrayed on brainyquotes) among many other quotes clearly show a reflection of the deplorable state of modern societies on a global scale. In case you do not know Pamela Meyer, she is an expert on the subject and thus her quotes were deliberately chosen after going through many other similar quotes. Pamela Meyer is in fact an American author, certified fraud examiner, and entrepreneur who was described by Reader's Digest in USA as "the nation's best known expert on lying," in the USA. If you thought the social and collective idolisation of lies was purely a Western world phenomenon practiced in the Western world, you would be mistaken.

These acts of accepting and protecting white lies (lies) is found in almost every known society or country, whether in the Caribbean, India, South America, the Middle East or Asia. In fact, in China, there is a common saying that stands as a soft golden rule in governing literally all aspects of communication and life among most if not all Chinese nationals and that is 看破不说破/ Kan po bu shuo po (which translated into English means: you see and hear something but in your speech or report or comment, you change what you exactly see to show respect and give face to another person).

To ignore this nationally recognised (unofficial) rule of communication, you will have trouble in Chinese communities or any Chinese society because by failing to compromise and go with the crowd, you will be regarded as unpatriotic, or seen as a very unsociable person who is too rigid, too straightforward and cannot live agreeably with others and have no mastery or maturity in proper communication and social skills.

Although it is proper to have restraints even in communication, are the current social norms we have settled on the best way to go about that? And if so, to what extent can someone bend the truth or bend reality to make the lie (false statement) acceptable and sound polite? For an unknown reason this question has not been answered and no rule has been set in defining or demarcating the extent to which one can go with telling a white lie (lie) or fudging an observation/truth/fact to show respect or save face and to give face to others.

As the fraud examiner Pamela Meyer already established, societies not only in USA but across many countries worldwide as we can observe daily, rely on lies to keep social dignity intact. What kind of dignity exists in your society and is it possible to dignify anything or have dignity at all if that dignity has to be kept intact and maintained with lies? That should help you better understand the next statement I will make. It therefore follows logically that society, with all of its good and bad, is still a construct built on lies. As a result, almost every single society needs more lies to be fed into it constantly for the purposes of order, sustainability and maintenance through various mediums including but not limited to government agencies, media houses and education systems. So it is of no wonder that the act of speaking the truth, standing against terrorism, evil and injustice within the society has all become a big no, a big faux pas and something not worthy of support but worthy of criticism and disdain.

If you thought there was some hope yet in religion and religious institutions, where morality ought to reign supreme, then you will be sorely disappointed to know that the last stand to serve as a beacon of hope for truth and morality and anything good and divine has become so infiltrated with corruption and lies to where these religious establishments all over the world are passively in some parts of the world, or actively in other parts of the world defending the status quo which is an elaborate lie and a big sham.

As a result, honest and sincere men and women suffer in society. You would have realised by now in your own life if you think back to past events that when you or others genuinely try to be as honest and transparent as a human can be, it always strangely backfires in your face and you end up being a loser, a victim or being the accused as the bad guy or girl (or gal, for those in Northern America). Every living human being has a small contribution to make in correcting the wrongs of the society in which they live and belong to. It is our collective responsibility to ensure and secure a better future for our children and those to come after us. The correction for a better world starts with the man or the woman in the mirror, each time you look into one (a mirror).

The following statements will shock too many since the place for teaching truth and right moral conduct is supposed to be churches, temples, synagogues or in other religious organisations. But once you go beyond the façade presented by religious groups and their representatives and examine the historical facts underpinning the message of hope and salvation, they are presenting to you or teaching you, you will be very, very perplexed or confused because of the incompatibility of sound doctrines and evil actions underpinning those doctrines.

The ubiquitous spread of religion and religious organisations came with many side effects including but not limited to terrorism, slavery, child trafficking and human exploitation. By feeding upon the right knowledge, being in your right person and right mind, all these things and much more becomes so clear, uncomplicated and simple to understand. It is well known today that religion has attempted and successfully controlled the minds of humans and nations through elaborate brainwashing and proselytisation for at least several centuries to date.

They have also risen to global power through continuous systematic hijacking, destruction and obfuscation of culture, historical facts and spirituality. Religious leaders and groups of religious bodies have also maintained the edge over other social organisation and institutions through the claim of fulfilling divine mandates, thus cleverly exempting all religious doctrines, sects and activities from sound, critical analysis or any human-based opposition.

Some religions have adopted militant and terrorist tactics to either murder in "holy war" or burn you alive or behead you, excommunicate you or demonise you in society through character assassination and false charges. Some use classic means such as threatening you with eternal damnation in the unquenchable hell fire prepared specially by the omnipotent yet all-loving god to burn in eternity all those individuals who dare to question the religious doctrines or its leadership. This has led to the encouragement and propagation of fear among the Masses especially believers. This inevitably leads to a growing population of fearful, fake, pretentious, docile individuals making up most societies all over the world. What then is the endgame here for those presiding over religious affairs in our societies?

4.1 Supremacy Of Religion Made Possible By Your Power And Your Money

Cats and dogs or parrots and other birds or insects such as ants do not have such a thing as organised religion but they follow the Natural Principle to live. People, however, have organised religion and they give their support, money, power and even spiritual energy to support and strengthen such a system of both organised and unorganised religions. So why would that same system, intentionally or unintentionally be used by others continuously for terrorism, corruption of the highest order, paedophilia, financial scandals, slavery, sexual abuse among many others unthinkable practices?

As a matter of urgency, where is the intervention, or when will be the intervention of that good and holy and just and all-loving, almighty god or deity (deities) who sanctioned these religious bodies and gave those prophets and religious bodies their holy scriptures and doctrines and to whom these religions are dedicated?

Have a quick look at this report published by the Guardian and the Observer in 2013. This report includes investigations on the attitude of the church towards victims that were abused by priests.

"The juxtaposition of those two images: the powerful institution that represents 1.2 billion Catholics, and the abused child, tells the story of a church with two faces: one public and one private. Last month, the church was plunged into crisis when the Observer revealed that three priests and one ex-priest had complained to the Papal Nuncio about Cardinal Keith O'Brien, Archbishop of St Andrews and Edinburgh. The cardinal, who publicly decried homosexuals as degenerate, had, they said, privately been making advances to his own priests for years. But the story was never about one man. It wasn't about personal weakness. Keith O'Brien was merely a symptom of a wider sickness: an institution that chooses cover-up as its default position to conceal moral, sexual and financial scandal.

This was not paedophilia but it was an abuse of power – a man in authority acting inappropriately to young seminarians and priests under his control. It was made clear that a full sexual relationship had been involved. Yet there were attempts to cloud his behaviour in moral ambiguity. First, there was denial. The cardinal "contested" the allegations. A day after publication, he resigned. The next week, he issued a statement admitting his sexual conduct "a priest, a bishop and a cardinal" had fallen short. Many ignored what that confirmed about the extent and duration of his behaviour: he was made cardinal in 2003".

Two concepts are critical to understanding church behaviour. The first is "scandalising the faithful". Traditionally, the hierarchy believed the greatest sin was shaking the faith of Catholic congregations. Protecting them meant concealing scandal. Adopting that as your moral standpoint means anything goes.

You can cover up sexual misconduct from those you demand sexual morality from. You can conceal financial corruption from those who put their pounds in the collection plate. You can silence the abused and protect the abuser.

Guilt about sacrificing individuals is soothed by protecting something bigger and more significant – the institution.

The second concept is "clericalism", a word used to describe priests' sense of entitlement, their demand for deference and their apparent conformity to rules and regulations in public, while privately behaving in a way that suggests the rules don't apply to them personally. (O'Brien was, in that sense, a classic example.) The Vatican is an independent state; the Holy See a sovereign entity recognised in international law and governed by the Pope. The Nunciature operates like government embassies in different countries worldwide. It is even governed by its own rules: Canon Law. All this contributes to the notion that the church can conduct its own affairs without interference or outside scrutiny. It demands a voice in society without being fully accountable to it.

In the weeks following O'Brien's departure, several priests' meetings were held in his diocese. One was chaired by his temporary replacement, Archbishop Philip Tartaglia of Glasgow, and O'Brien's auxiliary bishop, Stephen Robson. Some priests wanted messages of support sent to the cardinal, encouraging him to return to Scotland for his retirement. Compassion for a sinner? Or clerical cover-up? Some not only knew of the cardinal's behaviour, they may have been subject to it. "The clerical power structure not only protects clergy who are sexually active but sets them up to live double lives," says Richard Sipe, an American psychotherapist and ex-priest who has spent many years researching celibacy and abuse.

"Corruption comes from the top down. Superiors, rectors and bishops do have sexually active lives and protect each other – a kind of holy blackmail."

Is this the biggest crisis for the Catholic church since the Reformation, asked Professor Tom Devine, one of Scotland's leading historians? But one cardinal is not the crisis. Thousands of abused children around the world, and an institution that silences them: that is the real crisis. The church claims child-protection policies have been in place in Scotland since 1999. Judge them for yourself in the following stories. Events come right up to the last few weeks, with Keith O'Brien's resignation as backdrop. The American civil-rights activist, Martin Luther King, once said, "There comes a time when silence is betrayal." In the Catholic church, that moment has long since passed."

Notwithstanding the famous quote that 'God's time is the best', we dare to ask again, that where is the intervention, or when will be the intervention of that good and holy and just and all-loving, almighty god or deity (deities) who sanctioned these religious bodies and gave those prophets and religious bodies their holy scriptures and doctrines and to whom these religions are dedicated? This may sound too obvious but for the sake of every reader: did you know that there has never been such a time as this and there will never be another of this time as we end this era and move into a new era?

With all these experiences and happenings, what becomes of the relevancy of such organised system(s) of old and new religions and such religious bodies? And again, what is the legitimacy of the power and authority of such institutions and their subsidiaries in controlling the lives and affairs of innocent men and women and children of all ages?

Religion as we understand has done the unthinkable and monopolised morality and sanctity, which are essentially the two most important ideologies that govern human society and human relations. In the process of such a monopoly, religion as an organised system has now taken over and claimed all rights on the general principles concerning the distinction between right and wrong or good and bad behaviour. They did the unthinkable, monopolising divinity itself, claiming ultimate importance and inviolability, and the state or quality of being holy, sacred, or saintly.

This is evidently clear when you are raised up in a society where being religious gives you a blanket pass to high moral standing, notwithstanding your actual conduct within society. Yet to the unreligious, you are immediately judged and condemned by the same religious groups and individuals as an evil person, or an untrustworthy person of low morals once you openly declare that you are neither religious nor have any affiliation to any known religious body or organisation. This has also been a great contributing factor to the ever growing number of hypocrites in society, but that is another story that would require an entire book to do any justice to the subject.

Unfortunately, it has now become a norm in society, that any baseless accusations followed by sentencing and condemnations from the religious groups or zealots be meted out to those individuals unwilling to submit to, follow or associate with organised religious bodies.

There is no justice in this system yet it is the modus operandi of the established religious bodies of the day. The worst part of this reality is that while many have fallen victim and many remain oppressed (unconsciously or unwilling) under the iron-rule of religious bodies and churches, the supposed condemnation or sentencing and persecutions are blindly meted out by the religious zealots without the requirement of any substantive evidence.

That means as per religion, you (as a human being) are not free to choose whether or not to belong to a religious group, and the exercising of your undeniable natural right to choose who and what to worship as a free, natural human being is contemptuous in the eyes of religion and religious philosophies or principles.

Unfortunately, this sinister and divisive strategy by organised religion to divide humans and nations all over the world for economic, military and political power is increasingly becoming the order of the day in modern society.

Religion also puts invisible and visible barriers between families, friends, tribes, ethnic groups and nations and incite hatred which leads to wars and acts of terrorism, all of which are great impediments to global unity, human advancement and civilisation.

Fortunately, many who have come to the realisation of this great prevailing evil (organised religion) are forming a network of resistance against the old order of divine-tyranny religion imposes on families, communities and nations.

Through my journeys from Europe to Asia and Africa and living for years with locals from all known continents around the world, I speak from first-hand knowledge and experience and with great precision and accuracy that the artificial construct which is religion, has gradually over the years transformed free thinking beings into a hollow, submissive, fearful and obedient workers fuelled by fear of death and eternal damnation or losing rewards of better fortunes and happiness in the here and now or in the afterlife.

These religious followers and believers are constantly threatened and deceived or indoctrinated to believe that as long as they give up their individual will and accept the divine will of a deity taught to them by a designated religious leader or preacher in their particular religious society, they will have a free ticket to paradise and enjoy a wonderful life of riches in paradise after their death. Since no human is born a Jain, Christian, Muslim or Sikh, we will do well to ask ourselves a basic but important question. This will help us establish our position and where we stand in the grand scheme of things.

Although religion is riddled with more questions than there are sand grains on the beach, considering three of such questions will enable one become more focused, in identifying what needs to be done without being overwhelmed and disheartened with the sheer volume of unending questions needing answers.

First question: Is any human ever born with a religion from birth and what would be the sign or evidence of that baby belonging to the supposed religion with no parental or societal re-education and proselytisation into a specific religious cult?

Second question: How can religious doctrines that are supposed to be infallible, divinely inspired or direct revelations from holy, infinite, omnipotent, omniscient deities contain such huge amounts of irrefutable errors and glaring contradictions? And sometimes how can some of these supposed infallible holy books with divine protection be easily and successfully corrupted by finite, mortal humans who are merely creations of the creator who's Holy words they twist and change at their own mortal will?

Third question: How can infallible religious scriptures be correctly quoted or rightly inferred as the justification for evil acts, including enslavement of other nations, dehumanisation of women among many other atrocities?

So in all fairness and seriousness, holding no prejudice regarding this questioning, what in the world did we miss as a people, and how can there be all these recurring problems and questions, from generation to generation if it is really truth we all claim to hold dear and proclaim? Truth by definition is the quality or state of being true. Truth again can also mean that which is (rooted in) fact or reality.

Therefore, truth is only one and apart from it there is no other. So whatever you may talk about or referring to, for example, is in that moment true or it is not true, and there can be no middle grounds aside from that which is in reality. In this same way, we can say reality is one, and all others are but illusions and artificial creations mimicking that which is original.

Truth means that which is true, so we cannot maintain that we have different truths on the same matter or issue at hand, or else that would create a huge problem for those involved parties and for the entire human society, on top of all the many existing differences and problems we have to deal with day in day out. If we ought to respect and live in truth but everyone has a different truth on any important issue, then what happens when your friend or your neighbour's truth says that your truth is a lie? How then can one reconcile the truth and the lie to be at peace and in harmony? This is undoable. So invariably, Truth can only be one.

I am sure every single person reading this, would have either thought about, heard, or asked similar if not exactly the same question on religion and the state of being true in reality. Some may have even gone a step further to find some kind of answers in response to the above questions on the subject of religion, and the truth claims of the various religious scriptures.

We are all aware of the multitudes of existing religions in our societies and their strong and exclusive claims to having the truth or teaching the right way to God, the Cosmic Mother, Nature, or some other being, deity or destination. This explains why those born in India for example will be predominantly Hindu, Sikh or followers of the other major Indian religions, while someone born in China is going to claim to be Buddhist or Taoist, or follow Confucianism. The next-door neighbours to the North of China, are the Mongolians and the majority of them are followers of Mongol Shamanism.

Europeans or those born and living in the Americas may end up being Christians mostly while those born in Arabia will be Muslims following the religion of Islam and teachings of their prophet, the prophet Mohammed. Africans may follow their African Spirituality or traditional culture as their religion.

Another thing that always caused a lot of friction, created hostility and hate groups among many families, or within and among nations is the synthetic prohibition or taboo in many religious groups disallowing its members to enter into bonds, partnerships or relationships of any sort, or marriage unions with others not belonging to that same religious sect or faction. Even love is forbidden in the system of organised religion. The main reason for such cases can easily be attributed to doctrinal differences, where one religious group claims or sees itself as blessed and divinely chosen above the other humans, claiming divine supremacy or uniqueness and exclusivity over all others that do not belong to their particular form of religion. The problem only gets complicated from this point onwards as the other supposed inferior religions see themselves in the same light of divine correctness and supremacy over all other competitors and different or opposing religions or faiths.

These practices as we have often seen, so many times has led to religious and political conflicts not only in the region referred to as the middle east but also present in many other parts of the world including the Northern Ireland and People's republic of Ireland to this present day. It seems like the violence and all the divisions and misery that comes with the love and practice of religion has no end. All these religions claim to be the only, exclusive way to the one true God or true gods, even though their respective God or gods are all different.

Ironically, the God or Gods of these different religions with attributes of the creator of the world are all said to have only good peaceful, harmonious desires for humanity or at least for some chosen groups. So what is this rampaging madness and deadly rivalry we see every day amongst these same righteous and peace-loving religious groups around us and on media platforms? Yet a closer look shows that both fundamentally and superficially, some of these religious groups are very similar, while others are different with contradictory doctrines and belief systems, from the existence of God(s), to the non-existence of God, Atheism, Monotheism to Polytheism and so on.

The similarities and the differences paradoxically seem to be endless, leading the curious mind and sincere knowledge seekers down a bottomless pit riddled with confusion and despair. So who is right and who is wrong? This cannot be an easy topic for discussion under any democratic setting. This is clearly supported by the living evidence we see in the numerous conflicts within the European regions, America, Arabia, Africa and Red Sea regions as religious zealots fight for control over promised lands and Holy lands across the African regions, especially Northern and North East Africa which hosts some major and significance places of religious pilgrimages and religious sites of great interest.

The following tells the story of what happened between a non-religious person (an unbeliever) and a religious person (a believer) who were paired up in a car racing competition.

After a long argument on who would be the right driver for the entire race, the believer or religious zealot decided that he would be the driver since he believed that he was highly blessed and favoured by his God and that this would ensure the victory they both strongly desired. So the unbeliever reluctantly agrees to let the believer become the main driver for the race. The non-believer takes a rest, and the believer assures him they are in good hands just as the timer begins and the bell sounds for the commencement of the race. Not long after the race began, the believer and his partner were rapidly falling behind the other racers.

The unbeliever got agitated and asked the religious guy who was driving the car, hey man, get your act together, we are falling behind fast so better get a move on. The believer replied in a calm voice, "oh ye of little faith", to which the non-non-believer retorted, "dude, not again with this religious stuff, we are eating dust here man, and it has nothing to do with faith, it is just a matter of correctly changing gears and showing your driving skills if we are to win the race against these other drivers, so please let us get that done first and talk faith stuff after we get that prize money". The believer said nothing and just kept driving as he was earlier, glancing at his rear-view mirror now and then.

As per the time and speed at which they were driving, it seemed they were about 7 laps behind the leading group of racers ahead so the non-believer who was quite frustrated at this point after trying countless times to get his partner to drive as though he was interested in winning, bursts out angrily and says "why do you keep looking in the rear-view mirror? The other cars are all ahead of us and we are lagging behind, way behind by about 7 laps already so can you just stop looking backwards or upwards and just look straight ahead because all the other racers are ahead of us and we need to move, move forward".

To this the believer who is the driver replies swiftly, "bless your heart darling, but looking in the rear-view mirror, am sure you can also see there is a car behind us, so why not focus on the positive instead? I serve a strong and mighty God and he has promised me I will be the head and not the tail, a victor, and not a victim, a winner and not a looser, but you, my friend, are lost, you know your problem is that you are walking by mere sight but as a believer I walk by faith and not by sight and it would do you a lot of good to try exercising some faith, because without faith it is impossible to please God, and faith, my friend, is the only way to live in an atmosphere of miracles as we believers do daily.".

The unbeliever paused for a while then answered, "well dude, if you are going to work any miracles, now would be a great time because we have more or less run out of time and we are only halfway to the finishing line". Needless to say, they lost that race. Right there in this story, another problem emerges, the problem with the religious zealots, always in the habit of driving by using the rear-view mirror, a feel good sensation that numbs the individual from seeing what is ahead. For as long as you focus on the rearview mirrors and not the front view, you cannot know what is ahead and you will forever remain in the past, behind all the dreams and potential life waiting ahead for you.

4.2 A Historical Perspective

In terms of religion, which is said to be an opioid of the masses, how well does religious teachings do against the idea of success and logic? By having a look at the historical records and what is happening today in societies globally, one can easily answer this question of the deceptive, oppressive and imperialistic socio-political agenda and tactics that organised religion has adopted to give them an upper hand in all areas of society that matters. This has given organised religion and its creators unthinkable political and military power and the ability to accumulate a lot of wealth and riches.

In 585 AD, the Roman Catholic church decreed that women do not have souls. This teaching was later carried into America and it was taught by white missionaries that 'Black Americans' had no souls during the American dark ages and civil wars, when there was a massive move to convert dark skinned Americans into slaves using Christianity and other means including torture and force. So for many, accepting the Jesus Christ of those missionaries and crusaders really saved their lives, literally, whether that symbol of Jesus as the saviour was a lie or real.

For many natives, it was either you accepted the 'Jesus' being introduced by the aggressors and invading forces or you would be killed in the most horrible way. During the golden age of the Roman Empire in 585 AD and beyond, the church had many conquests and invasions or crusades to establish itself as the ruling class on a global scale in that era, all across Europe and beyond, with the Roman emperors being the head of the church or Christianity, up until the collapse of the Roman empire and renaissance that led to the rise of protestants and all other forms of Christianity we see today. Now in 1000AD, the same Roman Catholic Church decreed that 'noble men' had the right to rape peasant women without any legal punishment. So basically it was lawful and morally right according to the Church, to rape women as long as they were considered peasant women.

The above cannot be taken lightly at all and you can agree that it would take great pains and efforts for even a known terrorist group or tyrannical governments to pass and implement such barbaric laws because there would be some resistance or uprising in this age if such laws were publicly re-enacted.

Remember that, these atrocious practices and laws and many other similar laws were decreed and enforced by the same religious institutions that told the world that the creator God loved his creation so much that he sent his son to die on a cross in the world to save it from perishing about 2000years ago in calvary, Israel. Yet the same Bible records that the world will be destroyed by fire and a new world will be established, and that all those who refuse the sacrifice of the son of God will burn in hellfire for eternity. This may just be too much to take in and digest, as these accounts taken at face value are contradictory.

Ironically, it is a well-known fact, that, statistically, most of the (active) followers of the church and Catholicism are generally females or women. On the surface, these figures do not speak well of women unless, someone is doing a great job of hiding truth away from them and the public, obviously to the disadvantage of all females (girls and women alike). This has got to be the work of master deceivers; using subtle deception to keep the truth hidden in plain sight and for so long. You will do well not to take such matters and such organisations lightly for that mistake could cost you your life.

As you can see, most women of today who are religious engage in religious activities and doctrines whole heartedly, without reservations or any skepticism. They support and follow even to the point of death this same church institution that has been undermining their dignity and integrity while destroying their personhood for centuries. The same goes for men as well, but women unfortunately are at a much higher disadvantage on the whole. It is of no wonder that Denis Diderot, the French philosopher and editor-in-chief of the first Encyclopédia, said of religion: "The most dangerous madmen are those created by religion". Is there truth in what he said, or is this statement only a marginalised comment aimed at the extremists/fundamentalists in religious organisations?

Putting aside the many opinions from both sides of the argument, a look at the cause of the highest statistical records on global death tolls and its causes shows religion as the culprit. The many acts of terrorism, tribal conflicts and world wars being waged in society are all underpinned by religious tensions and have at their root cause, religion.

The fact is that, from its creation, more humans have died because of religion and religious conflicts than all other human conflicts. Religion on its own has destroyed more nations and killed more humans statistically than the damages caused by both world war I and world war II combined. That should make you pause and think carefully. Surely this cannot be a good thing regardless of the promise of a better experience and rewards in the afterlife in heaven or paradise by those gods who sanctioned these deaths through the divine messages, prophecies and instructions given to the various religious prophets and messengers. Instead of living in fear of any all-loving, obscure, partial god that may or may not exist, why not live right, live to the fullest of your amazing, yet unrealised potential and ability as a human being?

Why not spend that energy, time and money you invest in religious activities or churches into your life, to live in harmony with nature and your fellow humans and enjoy the rest of your life as you have it now, here on this beautiful planet without having animosity towards another person because they chose a different religious path to you? Would a good god anywhere in existence be against such a praiseworthy life? If yes, then it is clear, that, that 'God' does not deserve your admiration or respect, for such a being is not worthy of your worship and can never be responsible for your glorious creation. Just live, live your life to the fullest, and die empty.

Just by observing the nations of this world and current events, no natural human, with a good heart and of sound mind, can shut their eyes, ignore reality and emphatically claim that religion is the best thing that happened to humanity.

Those who might sincerely defend religion and praise religion are the few religious leaders, teachers and pastors/prophets who have become beneficiaries of the believers, living in multi-million dollar mansions and owning private jets and school complexes that have all been expressly and conveniently paid for by financial collections and contributions from religious followers, who are told to give on earth and reap their rewards in the afterlife. Such religious leaders or teachers living off the supply of the millions of dollars pouring into the churches would in all honesty continue the machinery of lies and deception as long as it continued fetching them their daily bread.

You would be a threat to them and their evil, parasitic style of livelihood and cut off their supply from flowing by teaching the truth to cause real self-empowerment and success for all those who cared to listen, believers and non-believers alike, religious and non-religious folks. At least one can say these pastors and religious representatives are living according to the law of 'the survival of the fittest' as proposed by Charles Darwin. It is important to understand the power that the game of religion wields.

Take, for example, the case of the omniscient, omnipotent and omnipresent attributes ascribed to the creator god in the major world religions of today. This God the creator who created you according to religious teaching in all the major and minor religious doctrines is omniscient, which means all-knowing and knows all things, past, present and future. He is omnipotent which means all powerful, and omnipresent meaning present at all places at all times and not bound by space and time for this creator according to religion created time, space and matter, and creating all the dimensions that comes with the universes, both the seen and the unseen.

Assuming the aforementioned statements are all true and accurate assertions, then this creator who created you gives you a free will to choose your own future. But this powerful and omniscient God should already know the outcome of your free will and free choices and actions, past present and future for he is all-knowing, all-powerful and not bound by time. If you argue that this God doesn't know what you will choose or do because of the free will you have been given, then that means the attributes assigned to the God as being all-knowing, all-powerful and ever-present are all untrue.

So why would a loving creator go through the complex or simple motion (for an omnipotent being) of creating you, with an end goal of putting you in eternal hellfire for eternal condemnation for exercising that free-will he gave you in the process of your creation in the first place, knowing ahead of time (as an omniscient, omnipresent, omnipotent God) you would rebel or choose a different path to what he wills to be done by you? Then what is the point of having free-will only to use it in following the will of another person or God, or totally submitting that free-will under the rule and will of another being or God?

The purpose of a free-will is to express it to the fullest, is it not? The key word here is 'free', meaning 'outside of the control of another', freely exercising that will outside or away from the control of another will.

Well, in an alternate scenario, if there is no free will, then it is even worse to assume or think there is a supreme being who simply creates humans to see them suffer in eternity in anguish and select a few portions of his own creation to enjoy life in paradise while the majority is destroyed or imprisoned in hellfire for eternity. Whichever way you look at it, it does not add up. Just try it.

By enforcing or declaring that a set of ideas or doctrines are not to be questioned, challenged or critiqued, you have in that moment destroyed free thinking or the right and freedom to thought and this is antagonistic to nature and the manifestation and expression of nature and natural laws. How then is this act any more moral than the forced mental or physical enslavement of an individual or group of individuals?

Another of the many puzzling issues with the fundamental doctrines concerning the origin of Christianity is the fact that according to many credible historians without political motivations or government support and affiliations, including the likes of Dr Yosef B. Yochannan, the exodus of the Jews or Israelites from captivity by Moses shockingly predates the father of all Israelites or Jews since the first Jew who according to Biblical accounts was called Abraham or Avram in Hebrew, was not yet born at the time of the exodus. Dr Yosef B. Yochannan, is one of the greatest contemporary Jewish historian and Egyptologist of the 20th century and early parts of the 21st century.

The rescue story of the Jews as a matter of fact predates the existence of the Jews or Hebrews themselves who were supposed to have been in captivity and needing saving. This makes no sense and is troubling for any group of individuals to know that there are some who out of greed and selfishness try their best to distort real historical facts this much just for their own gains and for power. This means the exodus of the present day Israelites or Jews as reported in the Holy Bible needs some serious revision if it dares to claim any historicity to such narratives.

But there is nothing wrong with this strange, impossible chronological order of such narratives and they do not require to be authentic historical narratives if all the stories told are just allegories to teach a lesson or promote an idea or an ideal. This is because if it is contested as a true historical fact, then it means the exodus of the present day Jews in Israel happened nearly three centuries (300years) before the first Jew even existed.

There has never been any recorded history of Egyptians enslaving a group of Caucasians who were called Jews in any time period to date. In fact, the only slavery in Egypt was the forced cultural and economic enslavement by several foreign invaders including Assyrians, the Achaemenid Persians, and the Macedonians under the command of Alexander the Greek, all of whom learnt and gained greatly from Egypt and thus settled and integrated parts of their culture with that of Egypt.

These are the real, proven and existing historical records and facts that no historian has ever attempted to dispute, and rightly so. How then can this be overlooked if we are all in our right minds, talking of the same historical account of a specific people in a specific time frame in the same world in which we all live? Is this lie flying as though it was a true historical account and not to be proven or questioned even in the absence of any evidence because of the threats and powers that back it up?

This is further compounded by the fact that the church also teaches that if you question Biblical scriptures and the authenticity of its doctrines, then you stand the chance of being burnt in hell fire as a hater or being proclaimed a demon-possessed unbeliever and a heretic, as was done to many in the past till today, especially during the times of the inquisitions and the Christian crusades. For the sake of the reader who may not know of what the inquisition or crusades were all about, here is a brief history on the two for your reference.

The Inquisition was actually instituted by Pope Innocent III (1198-1216) of Rome but came into effect under a later pope, Pope Gregory IX, who established the Inquisition, in the year 1233, in France. By 1255, the Inquisition was widespread throughout Central and Western Europe. The church had defined heresy as the act of free or independent thinking by an individual and making such free and independent thoughts or views publicly known or acting on them was punishable by death.

The official religious terminology often used to describe one guilty or accused of heresy is a heretic. Anyone found accused of heresy (freethinking) by the Church was condemned and sentenced at an Auto-De-Fe or as translated in English, Act of Faith. In simple terms, the auto de fe or Act of faith as it is commonly known, is a public torture ceremony for those condemned by an inquisition such as a Spanish inquisition, Portuguese, or French inquisition and so on.

An inquisition involves clergymen sitting at the proceedings of the accused to judge and deliver punishments. The condemned or guilty are those described by the inquisitions to be freethinkers (heretics), nonconformists or protesters. The inquisition would sit and decide whether or not you are a heretic (freethinker) and if found guilty of freethinking, you will be sentenced by the Act of Faith/Auto De Fe.

Most common of the punishments here included confinement to dungeons, physical abuse and other forms of torture. The most famous of all was the live burning of persons tied or bounded to the stake or tied to trees and people including the churches across Europe would usually gather as was the custom, to watch and cheer and laugh and praise their God and his only son Jesus at such event, for bringing heretics to the horrible deaths they supposedly deserved.

Some of the most common charges during an inquisition included the denial of the divinity or outright existence of Jesus the son of God, challenging the validity of any ecclesiastical doctrine, anyone publicly demanding historical evidence that proves the existence of Jesus or requesting evidence that authenticates the existence of other significant biblical characters. All these are considered heresy and punishable by burning those condemned at the stake. Those who reconciled with the church were still punished, but often tampered with some leniency. So even if you apologised to the church out of fear for your life, that was not enough and there was no such thing as forgiveness to be found in the Church or among the church elders, clergy and representatives of the various established churches.

Besides punishments, many others had their properties permanently confiscated or destroyed. Those who never confessed were burned at the stake as they screamed in loud excruciating pain. But for those who confessed and pleaded for forgiveness for their sin of free thinking or heresy, the Church tampered their sentence with a little mercy and thus were given the option to be strangled to death first, before being burnt slowly at the stake, saving them from being burnt alive.

So either way, once found guilty or even accused of heresy or questioning the teachings of the church, you would end up dying a gruesome death by being burnt horribly at the stake and be made a spectacle for the public to witness and cheer. This would definitely put fear in a lot and prevent many from the thought of questioning or seeking verification and authenticity of the ecclesiastical teachings and its origins and its relevance in society. During the 16th and 17th centuries, attendance at these stake burnings or as they were officially called, Auto De Fe reached as high as the attendance at bullfights.

The Crusades were a series of religious wars between Christians and Muslims started primarily to gain territorial powers and to secure control of holy sites considered sacred by both groups. Eight major Crusade expeditions were recorded to have occurred between 1096 and 1291. The bloody, violent, and often ruthless conflicts propelled the status of European Christians, making them major players in the fight for land in the Middle East and across Africa. This would later on aid in the wide and rapid spread of Christianity and Islam across Africa and neighbouring countries along the Mediterranean and Indian Ocean including India and also across South America and the Caribbean Islands.

In a nutshell, as the history shows, these and other tyrannical tactics used by the church and other religions has helped organised religion on the whole and its proponents to gain an outstanding level of political, military and economic power and a great number of followers. Now those who are still being exploited and victimised as believers or followers of the various religions have little defence in their favour for their active role or passiveness in their own exploitation and demise, because of the explosion of knowledge that can set them free should they desire deeply to be free.

A thorough understanding of reality and current affairs brings with it definite prosperity. Prosperity brings with it choices and competence, innovation and confidence and further development. This is clear in our world today, where about 40 of the most developed western countries in the world control a large sum (about 70%) of the wealth and resources on the planet, with the remaining majority, over 120 countries sharing the remaining 30% of the global wealth. As a result, most countries globally are counted among the poorest in the world, with high inequality gaps, famine, diseases, ethnic and religious conflicts and wild spread corruption.

It is worth noting, that the poorest regions, most divided regions and highly under-developed countries in the entire world are also the most religious regions in the world with Christianity leading as the number one most practiced faith in most parts of these poor regions. Is this strange reality a result of mere coincidence or the workings of highly organised and wicked principalities running things from the shadows?

As we all know, even drug lords, as heartless and wicked as they may be, would not allow their offspring/children to be oppressed and enslaved and forced to live in destitution generation after generation under his own employees or drug traffickers and agents working for this drug lord. So it gets really surprising when powerful gods who are transcendent beings as taught by the various religions of this world would allow their supposed beloved or chosen children and worshippers to go through torment and live under oppressive rules and become victims of economic hardships, epidemics, colonisations and genocides without doing anything or performing any miracle to rescue these beloved children, or worshippers. We have all seen or at least heard of wicked abusive parents rescuing and defending their children from other abusers though these parents themselves are guilty of mistreating their own children.

So how much more a supposed loving god who has more power and abilities than any abusive parent or drug lord could ever possibly dream of. So this cannot be a case of dealing with an impotent God, for God by definition is one with great and unimaginable power. Therefore, it is reasonable to conclude, that at best, this whole system and cabal could only be described as the fervent worshipping of an imaginary God, alongside Santa clause and others.

Concluding statement: Free your mind, Free yourself.

KEY 5: THE LAWS ENSHRINING CAUSES AND EFFECTS

"Leave him in darkness he who loves darkness."

Dr Ray Hagins

5.0 The Laws Of Nature And Your Role

Someone (parents, family, guardians, friends and society) may be responsible for what you are, but from this point forward, you are responsible for changing it. It is now general knowledge that we engage in mental activities with the mind and not the physical heart, which is located in the lower left part of the human chest, in contrast to the incorrect Greek philosophy which taught and postulated that the control centre of mental activities and emotions were in the heart.

The Mind is the control centre of mental and emotional activities and not the physical heart. The heart as well as other parts of the body are connected recipients of the processed experiences from the Mind. We know the heart has a very important role in the body. It is the muscular organ that pumps or circulates blood through the blood vessels to all parts of the body.

Remember that the statement about the heart and mind of a 'man' does not merely refer to men or males. In this context, 'man' is used as the generic term to refer to all humans, both male and female. Whether you are jobless, an ecologist or an economist, a legislator or administrator, politician or physician, parliamentarian or vegetarian, you can think, and the most significant and strongest existing barrier preventing you from thinking constructively and creatively is you (yourself).

Thinking is not reserved for a secret group of individuals, even though it seems to appear that way day in day out. Thinking is a human thing and has always been. This is the process that leads to the production of gods out of mortals. The only problem, however, is that most humans don't engage in this *thinking* business as some would call it. With a little thinking and reflection, one can realise and fully appreciate the existing strong correlation between a person's inner mental state and the external circumstances or life condition of that individual.

The well composed, well developed and focused mind will produce a more rich, productive and prosperous life, which is a true reflection of the inner consciousness (inner mental state).

In that same way, a confused, fearful, and anxious inner mental state will produce a poor, anxious, unsuccessful and frustrated life. The misplaced or misguided inner state will only produce a miserable, self-hating individual who has lost a sense of self-worth, with no self-pride and dignity and no self-love in their life. Such a person or a group with a lost and misguided inner self will often seek hope, an acceptance, a sense of belonging, worth and fulfilment by engaging in self-destructive behaviours or by following and willingly serving anything or anyone against their natural self-interest.

No amount of sacrifices, mediations, prayers, chanting or recitation of positive affirmations can be the solution to fix such a destitute life. You cannot bypass the already established and infallible spiritual principles enshrining the laws of causes and effects.

Many know about the physical law of cause and effect as observed in the material world in which we live. Although they know about the physical and material laws under which and through which we operate and interact with the physical world, they seem to have no sense of awareness or knowledge of the greater laws which govern the realties in which we are operating. For if they did, they would see, that as it is on the inner, so it is on the outer, as it is above, so it is below.

Until we set the inner state right, these countless life troubles will only grow to become a normal part of life, a life of failure and lack, a life of fierce competition and wickedness without remorse, where individuals live daily in the captivity, going so fast in circles with no forward movements or advancement.

Thus, it is far more helpful to you personally to think positively instead of thinking negatively about issues concerning you and life. Always do your best to use those empowering, uplifting positive thoughts as the basis for your actions, every moment, and every day of your life if you are to remain on a higher plane of living, where you too can finally live and enjoy the victorious life. Thinking negative thoughts will produce the negative experiences you dwell on mentally whether you like it or not, whether you mean it or not, whether you were only joking or not. Therefore, train yourself repetitively to think positive thoughts, form a habit of thinking positive thoughts and then act on those positive thoughts and you will enjoy the fruits of your labour.

Do not deceive yourself that positive thinking is thinking positive on Sunday after you have practiced negative thinking all week, from Monday to Saturday. You cannot think negative Monday to Saturday and think positive on Sunday at church and expect to enjoy positive results. The results you can get with such thinking will be nothing but frustrating, negative results. As the old African proverb goes, whatever a man sows, that and only that is what he shall reap.

Another common proverb of equal importance which gives a fairly simple yet accurate illustration to the law of causality and the phenomenon we are talking about here states that if you throw a ball against a wall, it shall bounce back to you.

So if you sow negativity with a little topping of positivity, you shall reap negativity with a light topping of positivity, or thinking negative thoughts all week and entertaining a splash of positive thinking will present a negative experience all week and if fortunate, you may experience a splash or hint of positive vibes in that week or the following week.

5.1 Freedom Of Choice

Note that majority of people relate to this world not in reality as to how things are or appear but rather, many see things as they think the things are and ought to be as per their personal knowledge or experience which they automatically and instinctively project onto that matter, person, thing or event. Therefore, two people for example may look at exactly the same thing but jump to two diametrically opposed conclusions, with each of these individuals claiming to be the one with the right conclusions and right understanding. An example is when two individuals are presented with a glass of water that is not yet filled to the brim.

While one person sees the glass as half full, another person will see the glass as half empty, thus approaching the same object from two polarised, contrasting ideologies. Usually, names we give to such folks in society is either a pessimist or an optimist, with the optimist having a more positive mental outlook of things and focus on only the strengths and desirable things while a pessimist displays a negative mental outlook, focusing on weaknesses and undesirable things.

Choose today which category you will to be in, to be a victim and a chaser of fantasies, or to be a victor, the master of your life, taking charge of your fate, because you have the innate power to do so. This is the secret to enjoying a life of success, full of blessing and peace that surpasses all understanding. Focus on the power of witches and wizards, generational curses, doom and gloom, and all the other abominable ideas and what you do is only fortify and multiply the effects of such abominations in your life.

You are free to choose what you want. Stop trying to force unknown spirits or gods to aid you in gaining riches or success and take actual charge of your life. Do not form a habit of trying to conquer mystic powers outside your reach to bring you riches. Chances are you do not have any power or authority in that realm or any other realm unless it be a realm or reality in which you live.

No amount of chanting, binding, cursing, hexing, no amount of deliverances, no amount of anointed materials, be it water or oil, charms or beads, no amount of fasting, praying and shouting or praying can bring you good fortune and success without you taking a conscious decision and acting to change your mental state and be in harmony with your natural environment. To deviate from this is to head directly for failure, to take the path of defeat and hopelessness. Sure some may use brute force to get one or two things they want in life and even achieve several goals of theirs, but that is not what I am talking about here. Such acts or tactics can never be equated to the principle of creative thinking and work that produces a real, lasting, and sustainable success.

The success put forward here is in other terms a holistic success, a success that transcends time and society. This is a state where you become one with the creative force and the source of life that sustains you on this planet. How can any amount of wickedness, greed, or brute force and deception put you in contact with such benevolence and magnificence? It is absolutely not possible, though some may try in vain.

Success is not a destination, as many believe it to be. To get that kind of lasting, holistic, and real success, you first need to work on your own self and on your mind. You either plan for life or life will plan for you. That is a very true statement, and this is beyond the feelings or beliefs of any single individual. You are now where you are because you planned to be or because someone planned for you to be there, consciously or unconsciously. It is not by coincidence that you happened to be where you are at such a time, and this is independent of what you may believe, what others may have told, taught or suggested to you on the subject of life and planning.

5.2 To Think Or Not To Think

Many are those who go through all kinds of unnecessary hardships and disasters in life. I chose the word unnecessary because that is exactly what their past and current hardships are, an unnecessary experience since there is available to them another path, another far better experience and a far better fulfilling life of abundance and joy if they had been guided rightly into it. This is the case and grim reality for many families and even nations, since the majority live life daily by seeing with their eyes without consciously engaging their brains. But that ought not to be so. To disengage your thinking faculties in life daily is simply to court death or regress actively into a struggle, chaos, oppression, poverty, and eventual extinction.

As humans, we are composed of both tangible and intangible substances or materials. You can see yourself as the perfect union of the seen and the unseen, the physical and non-physical. That is why you are so simple, yet so complex. This I guess is what may have inspired the old popular saying that humans are made of mind, body and soul, showing that the human is indeed made up of both physical and non-physical components. Therefore, we are sadly living far below our capabilities and limits if we live purely as sensory or carnal beings, being controlled by only our five senses on a biomaterial level.

We can be much more, and we ought to be much more if we are to survive what is ahead. Growth, evolution, change and progression are all natural phenomenon and thus the first mission, the first resolution, the first responsibility after gaining self-knowledge and achieving control of your mental state is to engage in all these listed processes.

To live solely for sensual gratification and pleasures of visual aesthetics has been the weakness of the masses, leading to a hopeless cycle of countless and endless untimely deaths, atrocities and conflicts day after day, year after year. This shows that to be carnally/sensually minded is death and by taking this route, you as an individual in one way or the other will pay the repercussions that goes with carnality and unmitigated dependency on the five physical senses.

One is not supposed to see with the eyes but one ought to see through the eyes, with the mind, to process, reconstruct and examine the information being observed. As you know, not everything that glitter is gold and you will be wise to remember that. This practice is the underpinning philosophy and principle of every successful human and anyone that may become successful in life as a living human being must stick to this primary occupation of thinking. By this method you can get much more out of life and that is the key am offering you here and now.

Nature affirms this key and by natural law, your eyeballs, for example, contain optic nerves, made of ganglionic cells which transmits visual information to the brain through electrical impulses for interpretation as you look with the eyes. This process helps you make sense of the visual event you just witnessed and it would be a great disadvantage and an unnecessary risk for you to consciously ignore thinking or disengage your mind from the entire process of visual observation. So seeing with the eyes devoid of the conscious mind is nothing more than a misuse of your optical apparatus, your eyes. This shows how important it is to think and not just to be under the illusion of thinking. Purposefully engage in thinking and you will not regret this endeavour as it will bring you great rewards and fortune.

To be under the false impression of thinking when you are in fact not thinking is even more devastating and dangerous than you can imagine, both to yourself and your dependants or those around you. It is a great disservice to yourself and an error you cannot afford to keep making. This is because to be deceived into or be under the false notion of thinking when you are not thinking makes it a lot more difficult to learn or take in and accept reality and facts. This is perhaps the worst form of incorrigibility and stubbornness or heard-heartedness which may be near impossible to cure once diagnosed, due to the inability or lack of self-awareness of the sufferer and the consequent unwillingness to see their errors or weakness and accept positive change.

The rare cure for this condition is a change of mind, a total washing as is often said, of the mind and reinstating the self as supreme in the subconscious and conscious units of your mind. That is the way to effectively manage and benefit from the ever-present principle of cause and effect, the principle of reciprocity. If you keep doing the same things over and over, you will surely get the same results over and over, whether you desire or like those results.

If you change your ways, your results will change. To change your ways, you start by making a choice to change your mind. This will produce different habits through repetition and then your results will change to align with your desires and that new mindset and new habitual way of living or that new culture. That is the complete road map, that few accept and follow.

Concluding statement: Free your mind, Free yourself.

KEY 6: RELEVANCE OF TIME

"The future belongs to those who prepare for it today."

African Proverb

6.0 New Day Comes With New Life

Today is the beginning of the rest of your entire life, so do well to make the rest of your life ahead count. You may have done well in the past or you may have failed miserably in the past. But like it is clearly stated above, all that regret or encounters of yours is now in the past, and today is a different day, a new start for you to do with it what you will.

The dawning of this day brings with it fresh, new and exciting opportunities you can draw from to change that unfavourable condition. This day marks the beginning of another opportunity for you to either start something grand or repeat the same mistakes of the past. So it is all about choice.

Making the right choice based on the right understanding of the knowledge and information at your disposal. You can consider each day you get as a gift or a present, and so today is your present to do with it what you will.

This is the present, and you are expected to maximise your potential in the present to the point where it echoes into the future. That is a big opportunity with an equally big responsibility if you think of it this way and you can make good use of such an opportunity.

To many, life is like a long journey. In the simplest of terms, we can liken the average human life to one who is engaging in a long, adventurous journey with a group of other individuals that may or may not be sharing the same ideologies and having different destinations.

If you do the easy things in life at the early stages of your life, you will have a seemingly hard life in the latter stages of your life. But if you endeavour to do the hard things that need to be done earlier on in your life, then you will have a much easier and fulfilling life in the latter stages of your life.

Thinking might not be easy at first, but it is what you need. Thinking is what you ought to train yourself to do so that it will come naturally to you and become a part of you. You have a responsibility to activate your mind and to use your mind. Some people have developed an addiction to powerlessness. So they are afraid of change in the direction of gaining power (and responsibility, since power comes with responsibility) over their own lives.

They are happy having no say or in-fact no final say on when they have to wake up, when they have to eat their lunch, or when to go for holidays and so on. They feel more alive if someone tells them when to sleep, when to wake up, how long to work or study and even when to fall in love and get married and have kids of their own.

They are also very excited when they are told or given permission to take holidays to enjoy themselves and spend quality time with their loved ones, friends and relatives.

They confidently claim and believe to be independent individuals or adults in charge of their own lives, yet they have no say and control over their time and absolutely no say how they live their lives and interact with others and their relations. They see this predicament as a normal life and a reasonable standard of living.

Whenever you get a negative report about your reasons for failing in something, whether it is an examination results from school, university or something else, remember that it does not refer to or say anything about your potential, because that report is only a reflection of your condition in the past, prior to your engagement in that activity. I like what Steve Jobs, creator of iphones and MacBook computers said in 2005, on the importance of life and time. He said, "Your time is limited, so don't waste it living someone else's life". This is a short and wise statement.

You can only live your life once and only you can live your life and live it to the fullest. So the best way to live your life is to be naturally successful at being yourself, and only you can achieve this feat.

You cannot be successful at being anyone else but yourself. When I say be yourself, I mean the art of being authentic, to know and be who you are and ought to be. Though you were young and didn't know what was happening as you were forced to do things in a certain way that was not beneficial to you, now is the time for you to take the necessary steps to correct those errors by any means necessary, to rid yourself of the bondages that has for years kept you disillusioned, bound in captivity and disadvantaged.

Now is the beginning of a new life, the time to enjoy the full expression of your new life. By getting this basic principle right, everything else will be in right perspective and things will settle in their rightful places in life. Then your life will be more meaningful as your impact in society echoes through the fabric of time, from generation to generation. This is a beautiful, worthwhile legacy. This is exactly what we refer to as immortality.

Through discussions with many of my undergraduate and postgraduate students coming from different walks of life and cultural backgrounds, I have had the greatest opportunity of understanding and seeing the world from many angles, through countless minds and diverse world-views and different cultures. This is another great advantage that comes with the profession of teaching at the university. By travelling around the world, I have had the opportunity to live and see the world for myself in more ways than I could have ever imagined if I had chosen to stay and spend the rest of my life in the city of London, in England without travelling the world. This again is a worthy undertaking.

Remember that what you think today will inevitably mould the life you see tomorrow. It is entirely up to you. You decide where you are going or better yet where you are not going. Whether you move or sit still, life is on the move, so you had better start moving if you are to enjoy the goodness and riches and happiness and fulfilment life has to offer.

6.1 Your Life Is Not A Joke

There is a world that has been pulled over your eyes to blind you from the truth and many have no idea they are actually under a spell. Life is spiritual and men and women alike are all spirit beings living inside physical bodies. I know that at this point, some clarification needs to be given and I will do just that. By this statement of life being spiritual, I do not refer to 'spiritual' in the same context as that of the commonly known mysterious, spooky, religious definition of the word *spiritual,* as taught by occults and religious groups or churches. I use spiritual here to represent something beyond physical matter, of something relating to the Mind.

This is a reinforcement of the notion that the essence of life cannot be seen with the naked eyes. I guess this is an obvious inner consciousness we all carry, knowing deep down we are spirit beings (non-physical beings) living in physical, biological containers called human bodies. To further explain this, we see the reflection of this knowledge in our culture and language systems and in the way we communicate with each other. For example, we hear no one saying, 'oh body is aching today, or arms are tired and body is not feeling so good today, or nose is running'.
Rather, we use a possessive determiner, 'my' to show that it is a possessor of the body talking about the arm or part of the body in question.

So you would in fact say, my body is aching and you will again say my arms are tired, showing that you are a being living inside a physical body and that physical body is your extension into the physical world, or you can call it your mobile home.

That is why we correctly say my body, with emphasis on the possessive determiner 'my' to show that an unseen observer is talking through the body about the body and not the body itself reasoning and talking. And in the same context, if someone has a cold, they will say 'my nose is running' and not say 'nose is running' or you could be asked by a friend where is your nose running to, and you both would have a laugh before correcting yourself.

Upon knowing this, we see and understand why thoughts, which are not material things can have such controlling effects on humans, from psychotherapies to hypnosis and many other mental activities or psychological experiments.

Your inner thoughts backed by that inner energy we call 'will' is that combination of power that inevitably controls your life. Whatever you will to do, will act to control and influence all your habits, whether that habit be good or bad. Therefore, it is of the upmost importance that we take the thought life seriously from henceforth and avoid self-depreciative thoughts at all cost. Instead, we can do well by continuously meditating on self-appreciative, uplifting thoughts that will bring us boundless edification both spiritually and physically.

The only true inferiority about a woman or man is the one the woman or man puts in herself or himself. Now at this point it is definitely worth noting that inferiority or a slavic mentality can also be forced upon you or any other individual in an unfortunate circumstance, through the instruments of education among many other forms, but, there is always a choice, an opportunity for exiting such unfavourable condition or a choice to remain in. It is all about the concentration or focusing of will power, to leave or leap out from that debasing condition onto a higher existence.

Have confidence in yourself and know that you have an active role to play in your own liberation. You cannot lay there, or stay on your knees wishing for someone to rescue you, for by doing that, you reduce your chances of survival drastically.

There is no such thing as a knight on a white horse, going around looking to save those in distress. That is a big fat lie, and at best a weapon that dampens or numbs your inner potential, so you had better wake up from that nightmare you call a fairy tale and face reality head on, by thinking your way to victory and success. Who said you could not do it? Of course, you can! If you really want to laugh, you can find some legitimate things and reasons to happily laugh about so do not fall in the trap of tickling yourself just so you can have the chance to enjoy a good laugh.

Even if you needed someone to help you out of your unfavourable conditions, whether you are afflicted by disease, death, oppression, enslavement or any other form of discomfort or torment, no saviour or hero in any form or shape can save you or lift you up without you giving 100% support and effort in that process. It has never been recorded anywhere in the annals of any civilisation or found in folktales or historical narratives of any tribe or nation stories of saviours miraculously saving folks without those oppressed individuals, groups or nations offering full support anyway they can to that saviour they are expecting to rescue them.

You were born to raise your head high and walk in style and grandeur so do not settle for less regardless of the current circumstance. Your current circumstance and those undesirable events are all fleeting away, so it is on you to do what you have to do to change the course of your life and enter a more desirable future. What are you waiting for? Just do it. There is no more a better chance, a better opportunity, a conducive time than the time you have now. You may be right in saying that what you are until now is no fault of yours, but that of your parents or whoever raised you and the society and conditions in which you were raised.

From here on out, and from this moment onwards, even as you read this, whatever you become moving forward now is entirely your responsibility based on your choices and actions. You have no business walking with your head down, drooping shoulders, and depressing thoughts. I call this attitude or nature the *dust-perspective*, meaning the individual or group sees nothing but dust and filth as they walk constantly through life, day in day out, year after year, with their head pointing to the ground, with an inferiority complex as their shoulders droop. You need not be like that.

You can do better and you can be better. The only thing stopping you is perhaps the know-how and enough focused will power to be better. And do not associate with people of this nature as this debasing mood and lifestyle or nature of dust-perspective is highly contagious.

Success is your inalienable right. To do something you have never done before, become someone you have never been before. You begin this by changing your mind, working towards mental renewal, which will lead to the transformation you desire or wish for. Give up what you have been or what you have become to enable you to become who you want and ought to be. That is the sacrifice you have to make, the cost you have to pay and a good sacrifice at that, to bring about self-realisation and complete success.

Stop trying so hard to hold multiple personalities and let go of those conflicts and sufferings you seem to have become accustomed to. It is time to let them go. It is time to let go of the chaos you have become used to, and to enter a new day of tranquillity and orderliness. You were born complete; you were born great, and you were born to live to the fullest. So stop settling for less and stop allowing yourself to be cheated, victimised, robbed, and manipulated as a hollow body or a hollow mass.

Sacrifice is giving up something lower we cherish for something grander, far better than the conditions and possessions we have and cherish. There is something far glorious ahead for you and that comfort zone you are in now. However, the current problem preventing the new world from dawning is the negative experiences clouding your judgement, blocking your vision and view from perceiving that glory waiting ahead of you, for you to step into. Just let it all go. Free your mind and free yourself.

You may have read or heard others say life is simple. As many have come to witness, life today is far more than simple, and if you joke with it, you will sink to the bottom like a big rock sinking to the dark and lonely bottom of the ocean. Make no mistake about that. If life were so simple, then why has it become so tough, so bitter, so difficult and so destitute for billions of people? Then I wonder what kind of life people would have to live and get used to if life was 'not simple', considering this so called 'simple life' has messed up a lot of folks and put countless individuals in bad shape.

But today I want to make it clear to you the reader, that life is in fact complex enough without the need to trivialise matters relating to life. Your problem in life is believing that old lie that life is simple, and then attempting to use simple tactics and plans to govern and live your life, which you thought or believed to be simple. But you will fail miserably by using this way and living by this false, deceptive philosophy.

Your life will become gradually unbearable and seemingly hopeless if you stick to this false, deceptive notion and philosophy that life is simple. Life is in fact complex enough as it is and you do not have to make it any more complex than it already is by refusing to wake up to reality and think. Life is complex enough as it stands. That is the simple truth to life.

Take charge of your thoughts and take charge of your life. After all, it is your life. Recognise this for your own benefit that neither the government under which you live nor the capitalistic, competitive, corrupt system can keep you from being successful as a person. Neither the star under which you were born, nor the poverty into which you were born, nor any disadvantages or deformities surrounding your birth can keep you from achieving true and meaningful success as presented to you in this book. The presented

KEYS are clear and concise for ease of understanding and have been carefully structured to allow for continuity of practice, which will inevitably yield the desired results constantly without exception. Nothing at all can keep you from having a fulfilled and successful life once you gain control and power over your very own mind and thought process.

When you enter upon the creative plane of thought you will rise above all the common, artificial barriers and become a citizen of another kingdom, the heavenly kingdom where you become what you were meant to become. Whether you are tired or not, nobody probably cares. What people naturally want to know is what you as an individual have or hope to offer humankind.

Your significance, lies within you and until you shine from the inside out, everything else will just be aesthetics and superficial and will pale over time, compared to your true potential in the grand scheme of things. Have a crack at immortality and become the man or woman you ought to be through self-realisation and self-edification.

Don't be like the kitten chasing its tail, running in circles after a class of cat philosophy where these kittens were told two things, that firstly cats are born to be happy, and secondly, that happiness is found in their tail. Rather do what you were born to do and that tail of happiness shall follow you all the days of your life.

Last but not least, remember that although somebody else may have been responsible for making us all what we are today, we are responsible for making ourselves become what we want to and ought to become.

Concluding statement: Free your mind, Free yourself.

KEY 7: UNPARALLELED SUCCESS THROUGH PURE LEADERSHIP (PL) AND CREATIVE THINKING

"You can surely go faster if you go alone, but if you want to go far, better go together as one group."

Christina Konadu (C.K)

7.0 Introduction to the Pure Leadership (PL) Model

Great leadership is key to group, national or organisational success. Global Leadership and Organisational Behaviour Effectiveness (GLOBE) is an organisation dedicated to the international study of the relationships among societal culture, leadership and organisational practices. With over 200 researchers from 62 countries studying over 17,000 mid-level managers in the initial phases, and its 2004 study being the largest and most prestigious study of its kind in the social sciences, the GLOBE showed a considerable influence of culture on societal leadership expectations and expectations for leadership effectiveness.

This shows a clear, strong correlation between the inhabitants of a society, their group mental state and the effectiveness of the leadership of that society. With their international, cross-cultural research and expertise coming together, GLOBE researchers studied leadership worldwide and defined leadership as "the ability of an individual to influence, motivate, and enable others to contribute toward the effectiveness and success of the organizations of which they are members".

I will give you a new definition for leadership under the newly developed leadership model called the 'Pure Leadership (PL) Model/Style'. Under the PL model, the definition of leadership incorporates the spirit and the essence of leadership in line with the success principles in the KEYS presented here.

Leaders, and in particular effective, legitimate leaders are unique individuals whether they are natural born leaders or raised leaders. PL styles are effective models of leadership that centres on a carefully balanced combination of the best human characteristics, values, abilities and skills. Such leaderships, wherever they may be found, can be identified as Pure Leadership and leaders fitting such exceptional and value-based practices are known as Pure Leaders. Pure Leaders are legitimate and trustworthy leaders who put their followers and the people they serve first.

Defining Leadership under the PL Model

Leadership is the effective application of an individual's abilities and qualities or traits in motivating, inspiring and enabling others to successfully accomplish a shared-set-goal beneficial to the group, nation or organisation to which they belong.

According to the PL model of leadership style, good leadership always go hand in hand with success and development, shared difficulties, shared prosperity, shared failures, shared victories and joyful celebrations. Pure Leaders are individuals who have great self-control and self-mastery. Such leaders are those who have conquered and subdued their emotions, making their emotions subject to them, rather than the individual being a subject of their own personal emotions and feelings.

Do not take self-control and self-mastery lightly, because there have been many kings and leaders of the past and present who have large multitudes or even nations under their control and have great responsibilities but cannot master themselves.

These seemingly invincible leaders with all their great conquests lack one major power, and that is the power of Self-Control. Many noticeable and devastating signs always follow such leaders who lack self-control and self-mastery, whether they be political, religious or otherwise. These signs include but not limited to acts of terrorism and the funding of terrorist organisations through open democratic means and subtle, covert means, invasion of foreign lands and sovereign nations based on false, trumped-up charges with support of heavy media propaganda and political rhetoric.

These listed signs, coupled with chaos, misery and misfortune, always follow such leaders wherever they may live. Another thing to note is that these noticeable signs may be given different names by these same incompetent leaders or elders (in societies or organisations or nations). It is unwise and unrealistic, by any responsible person to expect any incompetent, selfish and illegitimate leader to be incorruptible, bold, honest and have a sense of responsibility and love for their followers or nation.

Such leaders will never admit faults or errors and will allow no credible personality to gain influence or popularity under their rulership because they themselves know of their illegitimacy and incompetency as leaders. They need no reminding from anyone and they need not be entertained in such privileged positions of power because they are unfit for such privileges, honour and responsibilities as heaven and earth testifies to such reality through unexplained or unexpected natural phenomenon and other countless natural disasters and earthquakes.

Therefore, to maintain their illegitimate leadership roles and hold on to the power they do not qualify to wield, they either engage in a combination or all of the following tactics and strategies. These include renaming and redefining of reality with force, through armed conflicts or terrorism and other covert operations, recreate events and fudge facts and events or historical records and collaborate with local and foreign agents or entities and benefactors to maintain the status quo and keep things just bad enough to benefit them but not so bad to the point of revolutions by their followers or citizens, many of whom live as collateral casualties and victims.

Some of these illegitimate and faceless leaders and office holders also work hard against development and liberation of individuals and the Masses which they lead, either directly or indirectly, through subtle and skilful brainwashing by using such systems as education systems, economic systems, entertainment and media or social media to obfuscate current affairs or history, thus hiding the evil reality they have contributed to creating from being realised by the disadvantaged Masses who usually live quietly as innocent, tired, and underfed sheep being led to the slaughterhouse.

Such illegitimate leaders who seek more power and might without self-control and any balance often see themselves and their actions or ideals as just and something worth dying for (as long as it is not them or their family and friends doing the dying), thus often causing or engaging in international armed conflicts, manufacturing of wars, manufacturing and selling of weapons and isolating or labelling any legitimate regime which opposes their evil ways as the enemy that the masses come to fear and hate.

Such leaders always replicate themselves and their ideals or forms of imperialism through local and foreign agents who may take up leadership positions and establish economic or financial centres and banking groups around the globe, creating a massive messy web of conspiracies, puppet governments and puppet leaderships serving under these illegitimate puppeteers as most of the masses look on by in (passive/active) ignorance and go about their busy daily lives in total oblivion to the surrounding reality.

Below is a list of the ten visible major signs that follow these puppet leaders or elders in high positions.

1.Abdication of national sovereignty and resources to the puppeteer or puppet master.

2.Armed regional conflicts, wars, and rumours of wars.

3.Genocides and acts of terrorism, including the creation and financing of terrorist groups.

4.Creation of systems of corruption and institutionalised tyranny and systemic discrimination and injustice.

5.Destruction or unchecked sale of national assets.

6.Constant spreading of false information, causing social disorders, chaos, stress and fear among the Masses, with an extreme polarization of electorates.

7.Systematic and institutionalised mis-education and brainwashing.

8.Poverty and famine by creating a nation or system dependent on the large-scale exportation of raw materials and the large-scale importation of all kinds of consumable products and junk.

9.Rampant and progressive breakdown of natural family units in the society and nation while glorifying single parenthood.

10.Unchecked increase in economic misconducts, an increase in public debt and borrowing from foreign governments and private organisations with no recourse or sound planning and clear vision.

More shockingly, all these problems take place under these democratically elected leaders amid great wealth, abundant natural resources, abundant human resources and workforce, vast food sources and crops and abundant drinking water bodies. So the real question is not about greed or corruption. The real question here is whether the existence of such leaders can even be classified as lawful or morally acceptable even if they claim to have been democratically elected.

Aside from this, another important question that baffles the mind of any person or observer is how and why do the people, the masses and citizens allow such evil, illegitimate leaders to rule over them, or over any sovereign nation of innocent individuals who only want a chance to live in peace and harmony, pursuing their individual dreams and wishes? This shows it is easier to conquer a kingdom or nation than it is to conquer one's self. Many have failed in this battle, but you do not have to go down the same way. You can, in fact, change the outcome and re-write your own destiny so to speak.

In all you do, understand that your mind is your greatest asset, but it also has the potential to be your own worst enemy, if you neglect to take full charge and control over it. This is what that great old African proverb means when it says "if there is no enemy within, the enemies outside cannot do you any harm". Do not be your own worst enemy. Accept yourself and be one with Nature for you have been skilfully and wonderfully made. So let no one lie to you or tell you anything contrary to the fact that you are wonderfully made.

Acts of leadership can come from anyone within a group, nation or organisation. A leader is often a woman or man of great potential and power. Be that as it may, successful leadership needs the full undying support of the followers in that group or nation for the complete realisation of any lasting success in that group or nation.

Success in the group is not something of a privilege is to be privately enjoyed by the leadership alone. Rather, the enjoyment and benefits of the group's success is to be celebrated and enjoyed by all members of that group, society or nation.

7.1 Hallmarks Of Pure Leaders

Value based leaders are selfless leaders who bring better forms of living and expression to their countries, followers or those they serve and lead, instead of the commonly known leaderships that win the hearts of both rich and poor, suffering and oppressed citizens by selling thousands of promises and sweet visions of shared prosperity in the distant future while they enjoy their group or nations' collective wealth and resources in their lifetime.

Within a decade of its inception, this PL Model will become a widely preferred style of leadership globally in contrast to the popularly known and traditional styles of leadership such as laissez-faire or authoritarian forms of leadership that has always led to big issues of inequality, oppression and tyranny, discriminations, deceptions and wastage of both human resources and natural resources. With being a Pure Leader, it becomes very difficult and impossible for one fitting the description of a Pure Leader to lie and cheat or deceive others to maintain power and leverage over others.

Within this 7th KEY, traits and qualities or abilities essential to this new model of leadership is discussed. The PL model is a leadership concept that draws from positive psychological capacities and potential of the individual which when coupled with a highly developed organisational context, results in both greater self-awareness and self-regulated positive behaviours by the leader(s) and followers, thus fostering positive development for all instead of selective and nepotistic forms of development that creates severe and systemic inequality among groups and nations under current standards and models of leadership.

The marvel here is that the Pure Leadership style of leadership is contagious, in that, the traits of a Pure Leader inevitably draws out the strengths and best potentials within each member or follower under that Pure Leadership or Pure Leader. This means that Pure Leaders will be those leaders we seek, those leaders who will lead with purpose, charisma, vision, right values or morals and integrity. Such leaders bring about positive changes and transformation, the exact things this current world needs.

As Karl Marx once said, "the philosophers have only interpreted the world, in various ways; the point is to change it'. Adopting the PL model or supporting Pure Leaders will bring about that desired and long awaited change. This process of change may involve changing personalities, mindsets and harmful and pointless foreign or local cultural practices to allow for development and growth. In this way, we can accept that positive and beneficial change is definitely difficult to accomplish but far better and worthwhile than the option or choice of doing nothing. Change is a serious business, especially one that involves a few or more individuals. It is not a joke or something to be taken lightly as one would a one-liner comment.

In a world plagued with corruption in all thinkable forms, financial crisis, pandemics and global terrorism and conflicts, widespread public dissatisfaction and fierce competitions, what we really need is such Pure Leadership, to bring about the long overdue transformation we have been waiting for. Without Pure Leadership, this world will soon implode, or simply retreat into an era more terrible than the historical dark ages.

Although PL is not something for every individual, having an awareness of these traits and abilities will still be beneficial to you personally and even help you make better and informed decisions or right choices whenever necessary and wherever you may find yourself. With that said, let us now consider on the following pages a summary of 14 abilities or traits that makes a Pure leader under the Pure Leadership Model/Style.

According to the Pure Leadership model, Pure Leaders are key to group or national success. Therefore, let us take a moment to read and reflect on who or what counts as a Pure Leader and some key attributes, qualities and skills a Pure Leader possesses.

Traits of a Pure Leader under the PL Model

The first trait under the PL Model is self-awareness.

Self-awareness is a key ability that every Pure Leader possesses. Being self-aware makes up knowledge of one's self and also the complete awareness of your duties and responsibilities. Mastering self-awareness means the individual knows about their history, condition and can rightly discern where they are, where they ought to go and what needs to be done to make the dream or plan a reality which will benefit more than the single individual. This is because without the group, there truly is no self, and without self, there can be no group, for all have but one source, and out of unity comes diversity.

All is one yet not all are equal, and each is a unique expression of the source. The Source is the one true Nature, and the one true Creative Force that exists and permeates through the ether in this universe and beyond.

Self-control or self-regulation is the second major trait after self-awareness.

From the understanding and development of self-control, one can empower herself or himself and show the wonderful ability of controlling and managing their own emotions and managing the emotions of others in the group, nation or organisation to which they belong.

Knowing and managing your emotions and motivating yourself are all key endeavours ensuring an effective leader who will thrive in both the good and the hard times. This means such a leader who has mastered self-control can perform competently under pressure, and deal calmly yet swiftly in times of emergencies while possessing and showing the impressive ability to meet impossible deadlines and complete impossible tasks.

The third trait you need to be familiar with is Effective Communication skills.

This kind of skill involves developing or possessing effective speaking skills and being an active listener. You can only communicate well if you can listen and hear and understand well. Here, any Pure Leader and effective leader will have to be an exceptionally good communicator.

The successful leader under the PL model should be a good communicator who can articulate effectively and communicate their visions and missions to their followers and other key stakeholders and to the public in clear, concise manner, without the use of unnecessary jargons. I see this as a great necessity for any effective leader and most charismatic leaders excel in this area as they can captivate their followers and the public usually through their personality or speeches, backed by their convictions and auras. Leadership failures can in most cases be attributed to a breakdown in communications at various levels within a nation, family or group. As a result, we cannot stress the importance of communication in leadership.

The fourth trait is decisiveness.

Any Pure Leader must possess the trait or ability of being a decisive individual. This proves the effectiveness of such leaders. One who doubts or hesitates is like a wave on the sea, tossed back and forth by the winds. Any indecisive, two-minded leader is dubious, irresolute, unstable, unreliable and uncertain about everything. This is the reality we have to wake up to, because wishing it away or redefining it in a more politically correct term will not change this reality.

So better to deal with reality effectively instead of playing the game of pretence and illusions. To get anything accomplished effectively, decisiveness and effective action is needed, not ineffective, superficial decisions that sound good to the ears and appeal to the emotions. You must be decisive and know where you and your group, nation or organisation have been, where you are and where you are taking the organisation or followers, you are leading.

An additional quality a Pure Leader must possess with decisiveness is being in touch with their emotional intelligence(EI) or emotional quotient(EQ). This will help them make better judgements and tougher decisions, which are all key ingredients to leadership success and consequently to organisational or national success.

Indecisiveness itself shows a sign of lack of self-confidence and that the individual is not sure of him or herself. How then can such a person lead effectively? Thus, the matter on indecisiveness is decided! Such a leader is not one to be followed. Such a person needs help and is in no position to help or offer leadership to others.

The fifth trait of a Pure Leader is the ability of horizon-scanning and detailed-scanning.

A Pure Leader should be able to perform a horizon scan and go into details whenever required to get the job done. This ties in with components of self-awareness and elements of Emotional Intelligence or EQ.

Being aware of both the bigger picture and smaller details ensures an outcome specific approach to leading as the leader proves she or he knows of where they are as a group where they need to go as a group (destination) and what is needed to achieve that which is to be achieved (the solution, dream, goal, targets or destination). In the same way, the leader will also be able to identify problems and provide solutions to those problems to ensure that goals are met and tasks completed successfully.

This ability also helps the leader to foresee or anticipate future risks and threats or potential problems and work in advance to avert or avoid such threats and hindrances from becoming road blocks or from materialising into active problems that will impede progress of projects and completion of other tasks or programmes.

The sixth trait is a compound trait consisting of multitasking and clarity of purpose.

These traits and abilities are better off going hand in hand instead of possessing or exhibiting just one half or the other of this compounded trait. The leader must be a multi-tasker while possessing a clarity of purpose. This means immunity to distractions and unnecessary deviations in a world with a daily bombardment of opinions and gossips, superfluous education and unproductive information or redundant knowledge that holds no truth and brings no edification to the consumers and seekers, listeners or students at the receiving end.

On top of being able to manage and skilfully execute or oversee multiple tasks, the effective leader will have immense concentration and focus on the task(s) ahead. This ensures the successful completion of tasks, then progression onto additional tasks which will add value to the organisation, group or nation. A leader with clarity of purpose will be highly functional and goal-specific or mission oriented. The leader possessing such qualities cannot fail.

The seventh trait of an effective leader is a leader with a sense of justice and fairness.

The effective leader has to be fair in judgement and also fair in his dealings with others. He must be objective and factual in his actions and decisions and not be partial or biased. The opposite of such leadership is a leadership that indulges in deceptive means and corruption. They accomplish this through cheating and spreading lies and defending those lies as though they are facts and by so doing take away the power of the many people who will believe and follow them.

As this deception goes on, these cruel and illegitimate leaders engage in the continuous process of feeding on the energy of the Masses, simultaneously keeping the masses docile or asleep and sluggish through structured and systematic brainwashing and many layers and levels of bureaucracy and carefully structured hardships as a normal or standard way of life. Such hardships and unnecessary bureaucracy dumped upon the masses may be seen by some as an unfortunate condition to put a person in, but this way is the most effective way of devising diversionary tactics which efficiently prevents the Masses, groups or nations from waking up to the grim reality of their oppressed and slavish state or conditions.

By preventing them from realising this truth about their own personal reality and life, the individual who forms a part of the Masses and finds their identity in the Masses will definitely be unable or will have no time to think or have any strong and focused will and desire to change their condition or remedy their situation. Let us be weary of such desperate and destitute individuals who seek to be a part of us or those broken ones are already in leadership positions seeking to engage in business or commerce with us. They may even come bearing gifts, but we are already immune to their trickery and treacherous ways.

The eighth trait is that of being a visionary.

The successful leader must have foresight and insight. Much can be said on this quality. The effective leader must be a visionary. He or she must possess the ability to see the good in others without focusing too much on the negative side. Instead, the leader should focus on the many positive aspects and potentials that could be developed.

The visionary leader is one who can think beyond the normal and see ahead or see through time to produce successful plans that can withstand the test of time and the changes that comes with time. The greatest visionary leaders are the ones able to work out things so far into the future it seems nonsensical, and their ideas or projects and its practical outworking seems so absurd and impossible to their comrades and the ordinary person.

Because of their amazing quality, visionary leaders are often misunderstood in their times or era in which they live. Because of their exceptional and extraordinary abilities, visionary leaders are usually dubbed as 'crazy' individuals or 'lost-touch-with-reality' individuals and they are only hailed as saviours or heroes many generations and even centuries after their death, once the successive generations have caught on to the century old ideas, projects, plans or visions of those visionary leaders which once seemed like madness or absurdity during their inception.

This is because these visionaries can see far into the future, and replicate a practical idea or vision that efficiently fits into the current society and future societies, with the implementation of such ideas and projects seamlessly solving current and future problems with no significant inputs from the future generations as they enjoy such impressive projects and ideas far ahead of their time.

The visionary leader can usually produce such practical and futuristic idea or projects after witnessing and assessing the current circumstances from undertaking or conducting a successful situational analysis.

The ninth trait is integrity.

This is a trait that allows the leader possessing it to command trust and to be trusted. Not much is to be said in defining this quality as we fully know of the meaning and importance of integrity as a character in an able woman or man. Integrity in a man or woman is self-explanatory, and it is something you either possess or not, and there can be no middle place and no compromise with this trait, as with all the other listed traits and abilities. The Pure Leader is a man or woman with integrity.

To be recognised as a Pure Leader, one must possess this trait and not be willing at any point in time or under any pressure or circumstance sell or trade this trait for anything on earth or in the heavens. This sets the Pure Leader miles apart from all other leaders and means any Pure Leader can function effectively with no compromise, no matter the temptation that may arise or any conflicts of interests that may arise, be it bribery or inappropriate and unethical material gains.

The tenth trait is honesty.

Honesty guides good people, but dishonesty destroys treacherous people. This is self-explanatory and the honest leader will act honestly at all times. Honesty develops trust, which enhances communication and strengthens relationships. Exhibiting this trait is a sure and effective way of building a solid, healthy relationship with followers and ensuring a stable, loyal and productive team working together towards a common goal.

The eleventh trait is selflessness.

The selfless or altruistic leader is an empathic and caring leader. Such a leader is also an active listener who acts solely in terms of public interest, winning the trust and support of followers, who will support and follow every directive from such a selfless and genuine leader.

The twelfth trait on the list is openness and accountability.

The leader must be open, accountable, and always willing to take full responsibility for any results or the lack of it. The effective leader must act and take decisions in an open and transparent manner and be accountable to followers under his or her leadership. These practices will ensure a deeper trust in leadership and thus a favourable atmosphere for development and growth.

The thirteenth trait of a Pure Leader is great will power and great resolution.

Great Will and Great Resolution is essential as these together provides a pushing force to see things through, to get done the things that must be done even in the face of strong and wicked opposition. These traits are natural way makers, and whenever there is no way, great will and great resolution will make a way for the one who possesses them.

The fourteenth trait of a Pure Leader is great Love and Passion.

Love which is the last trait here is a force that acts as an invisible adhesive, pulling together and maximising all the effects and powers of the other traits together in perfect unity, producing a synergic effect in Pure Leadership. Love is the unifier that brings all the listed great traits and abilities and skills together, to produce the exceptional leader, that is the Pure Leader. Love is kind, love is faithful, love knows no hatred, love is strong, love is discipline, love protects and honours, love is not self-seeking, love is forgiving and love is just. Love does not overlook wrong doings and love is definitely not blind.

Love holds onto and promotes that which is good, and hates and repels that which is evil. Just as it is with Love, Passion is another great positive feeling towards something that is deeply and personally meaningful. The Pure Leader is one who is passionate about the vision, and just as it is with love, this passion generates energy, excitement and enthusiasm. Great Love and Passion are the abilities in a Pure Leader that inspires others to happily and willingly join and identify with the leader's vision.

7.2 Attaining Success Through Creative Thinking

Creative thinking involves the creation of new ideas and so on, as explained earlier. As stated earlier, any nation, group or organisation under Pure Leadership will benefit from creativity and innovation, as these abilities are major traits to all Pure Leaders. In any group, nation or organisation for example, creative thinking is a vital tool in ensuring not only the success of that organisation but this practice will also allow that group, nation or organisation to excel and lead the particular field in which such a nation or organisation enters.

Creative thinking which births excellence and innovation is usually easily crushed or hampered by common and seemingly trivial practices that may include any combination of the following:

Trivialising significant issues, failure to brainstorm where necessary or failure to engage in the practice of exchanging ideas with like-minded comrades, overlooking problems, choosing efficient but old and well-known routines over innovation thus creating and operating from a position I refer to as the familiar zone, overworking or excessive physical labour, excessive and undue strict adherence to old formulated plans, passing the blame or shying away from responsibilities and promotion of unqualified personnel or individuals from within the group, nation or organisation under the pretence of loyalty and internal policies.

Although there are other mistakes that hamper creative thinking and innovation, these are the major common blunders that usually inhibit or totally extinguish creative thinking or creativity leading to failure and underdevelopment. Agent Smith from the Matrix movie reiterated the affirmation that many humans living in the world are using all their muscles except the muscle that matters the most, when referring to the use of brain cells or mental muscles for thinking your way out of trouble and desperate situations. This mind agent Smith spoke of in the Matrix movie is a possession common to all humans. However, this possession is the most heavily under-used possession among many humans living today.

As a result, many end up with nothing but a life of defeat and failures, surviving by hand to mouth, on a daily, weekly or monthly basis, with unimaginable pain and suffering, afflicted with poverty and diseases, instead of rightfully taking their places as faithful stewards of the planet and divine heirs of the cosmos with dominion over all of creation.

All these things and similar unfavourable circumstances can be changed simply by exercising our thinking faculties, using our minds and thinking with our highest faculties. Then and only then can we as a people, as a group of living beings, take our rightful place as gods, as children of the most high God, and become one with Nature. Failure to assert mastery over your lower self, which seeks the instant gratification of the senses, will lead to catastrophic failure and death.

Concluding statement: Free your mind, Free yourself.

KEY 8: DUTIES TO SELF - THINKING YOUR WAY TO COMPLETE SUCCESS

"You are what you think, and the secret here is that your life is exactly what it is because of your own mindset or the lack of it. If you look in that mirror tomorrow morning and don't like what you see, then know that you have a lot of work to do, on yourself. The mind is in fact the architect of your life."

Felix Bassuah

8.0 Thinking Is A Personal Responsibility

Someone (parents, family, guardians) may have been responsible for what you are; you are responsible for changing it. Build great relationships with people that will constantly build you up and raise your bar of achievement, with those that will push you forward and encourage you to challenge yourself. Be careful who and what advice you listen to and be extra careful concerning the credibility and integrity of the source of the information or knowledge you regard as fact.

According to the laws of aerodynamics in physics, a bumblebee for example is not supposed to fly because the wings are too tiny to support the disproportionately huge body, but reality is that the bumblebee as an insect is not aware of the scientific fact it is incapable of flight. And guess what, bumblebees fly with joy, against the scientific order of the day. They just take off in flight using those tiny wings said to be scientifically incapable of flight. It enjoys a whole new world that can be appreciated only through flight and by living on a higher plane of existence. So take a calculated risk and grow beyond your wildest dreams.

Build yourself and refuse to live from hand to mouth. Have the uncommon desire to control your destiny because it is your destiny.

Thinking is without a doubt the highest form of human activity. So how come thinking is very much neglected in our day-to-day life activities and few are acquainted with or even dare to engage in this art of thinking? How come this essential art or activity of constructive thinking is totally neglected in all forms of formal education all over the world, from the so called developed worlds to the so called underdeveloped worlds?

How come there is no room for the teaching and the practice of thinking? Is thinking troublesome and that useless, and not even worth the effort of our consideration as humans? Or could it be because it is so precious and priceless that we have deemed it worthy to reserve such a glorious activity (thinking) for a selected few? As the saying goes, nothing is as approved as mediocrity; the majority has established it and it fixes it fangs and claws on whatever gets beyond it.

8.1 The Amazing Human Mind

On this subject of the mind and success, William Shakespeare asserts that our doubts are traitors and make us lose the good we often might win by fearing to attempt. In this situation, experiences will speak louder than opinions on what doubt may or may not have done to you or for you, in your personal relationships and everyday life activities. In Revolt of the Masses, the Spanish essayist and philosopher Ortega also made some assertions along similar lines. He puts forward a convincing argument that described the masses, and attempts to separate uniqueness from the ordinary or commonplace. He argues that strictly speaking, the mass, as a psychological fact, can be defined without waiting for individuals to appear in mass formation.

In the presence of one individual, we can decide whether he is "mass" or not. The mass is all that which sets no value on itself -good or ill- based on specific grounds, but which feels itself "just like everybody", and nevertheless is not concerned about it; is, in fact, quite happy to feel itself as one with everybody else. The characteristic of the hour is that the commonplace mind, knowing itself to be commonplace, has the assurance to proclaim the rights of the commonplace and to impose them wherever it will. As they say in the United States Ortega writes, "to be different is to be indecent".

The mass crushes beneath it everything that is different, everything that is excellent, individual, qualified and select. Anybody not like everybody, who does not think like everybody, run the risk of being eliminated.

Our mind is that part of us that connects us to God, the Ancestors, the natural world, the unseen world with all of its unseen realities or whatever you may call these things in your culture. With this I will go even further to conclude that the mind without a doubt is an invisible force or otherwise known as a spiritual force. Do not be shocked by this bold statement I make, because things will become clearer as you read further.

This book is not written to establish whether or not there is a God (Transcendent being), for that fact has already been settled. The only statement I will add here to support the Unseen force is that since we are finite beings, there existed a First Cause, that which pre-existed the humans, that brought us into existence and to deny this basic truth is to deny and invalidate your very own existence as a living, thinking being.

There has been many attempts to quantify or qualify this magnificent Cause (Power) that gave birth or produced us and some given titles, the many names or attributes, include but not limited to God, Uncaused Being, a Transcendent Being, Infinite Mind, Universal Being, Universal Mind or Mother Nature and so on.

You had a cause and that first cause or entity that brought about your existence is what you or others may refer to as God or gods and so on. Nothing can change unless we change and we can never change unless we attempt to see things differently from the way we used to see things or see things differently from the way we were taught or conditioned to see things.

According to findings from several researches by world leading scientists in the fields of neuroscience and quantum physics, our experience of the physical world around us is far more complex than we have previously been made aware of. No one seems to know how humans can have epistemological experiences or concepts. This is because although thoughts and thinking arise from the brain, we do not know the exact mechanism or physical portion of the brain, which makes thoughts or thinking possible.

However, there is no doubt about the certainty of thoughts, thinking and human perception and intuition. Such things as thought, perception, and intuition are all daily, concrete parts of our lives. Yet it is interesting to note that it is impossible to recreate or proof such things or such realities scientifically in the laboratory as one would observe and replicate or repeat the vaporisation processes of a block of ice using a fire or the distillation of crude oil to get petroleum and kerosene products and other exact results as expected each time. We may not be able to use some chemical reactions or material science to reproduce such realities and experiences but the inability to do this does not in any way negative or nullify the fact that these functions and mental activities are a part of us.

Since we cannot see or observe the art or process of thinking on a machine, we know that it cannot be simply classified as a physical activity. While most humans are unconsciously or subliminally aware of the fact that, we as humans are non-physical beings living in a physical body, some humans have achieved conscious awareness and understanding of this same fact. As a result, those who know of this fact consciously tend to live their lives by such insight and any individual who falls into this category is often regarded as an erudite. Others take advantage of this insight and apply such knowledge in ways which gives them leverage and higher standings in their dealings with others and the world in which they live.

The inability to physically see and observe the Mind produces a great fascination. Along with this fascination comes many theories and questions. The quest for the identity of the unseen, non-physical observer in our physical body and brain responsible for the act of thinking has led to several investigations into the cortical and sub-cortical regions of the brain in an attempt to make sense of these wonderful phenomena. Unfortunately, all such investigations on a worldwide scale have failed in identifying who this unseen observer is in the human brain or body. No scientific discipline of today has been able to identify how this occupant came to be.

Scientists throw up their hands in the air at this point while others attempt to push their investigations further in search of a reasonable answer through religion and mysticism. This only goes to further affirm the assertion I made earlier in defining the mind as a spiritual entity, our spiritual core, that serves as an interface linking us to the infinite power, Nature, the cosmos, or to God, depending on how one may choose to refer to such magnificent power. The mind we possess is not a physical material to be played with or labelled for experiments.

8.2 A Mental Paradox: I Think I Cannot Think

Having established thinking to be so important, why have so many people neglected to engage in such a vital activity? Well, the answer is simple! This is simply because thinking really is the most difficult and yet most fundamental activity a man or woman can engage in or perform. Some philosophers have stated that 'I think, therefore I am'. Well, I dare go beyond this and reduce this to a simple, observable fact that 'I think therefore I matter, and you do not think therefore you do not matter'. After all, that is the total summation of the current situational analysis of our world we live in today.

A few conglomerates and a few well-organised families for centuries now have been gladly doing the thinking and educating for the masses who gladly and proudly follow without a thought. For if many individuals had but a single original thought, they would turn away from the sinful, unproductive fierce competition, hypocrisy, systematic enslavement and subtle yet pervasive dehumanisation of the individual human being and their personhood.

It is without a doubt a daunting task for a few clandestine organisations, a small group of individuals or even one nation to covertly or overtly take on the huge, global responsibility of leading the rest of humanity. As we all know by experience, with great responsibility comes great power. And what in this world would you say can be more dangerous than great power in the wrong or illegitimate hands?

The continuous existence of the evil, predatory global systems and their shadow-leadership groups have all been made possible through repetitive formal brainwashing-curriculums at formal institutions and education centres, through religious indoctrination at churches and proselytisation, and the constant broadcasting of false information by carefully developed media platforms and often well-trained puppets, so-called secret-agents and intelligence agencies.

If any authentic, charismatic leader, a public figure or superstar attempts publicly to go against such well organised evil institutions in an attempt to free the subjugated Masses, they are often met with a twisted fate, met with all forms of false vilifications and character assassinations from those evil Organisations clinging to power on top of betrayals and misplaced hatred from the same oppressed masses they intend to free or fight for, bringing these well-meaning saviours and heroes or heroines to their untimely demise while putting off other would-be saviours from attempting any rescue missions on behalf of oppressed nations.

These same masses will go on another strike, public protests and so on from time to time, to cry out for justice, equity, fair wages, equality and freedom while betraying anyone who seeks or attempts to offer them a helping hand out of their deplorable predicament.

Sitting back, one may wonder, what at all does the public or the Masses want? What does the Mass want? We can only wonder if this is some kind of malady, a diseased state in which the oppressed develops an unhealthy addiction to their oppression or the poor and hopeless develops an addiction to their poverty and hopelessness. In such cases, the individual sufferer or group or nation under this deplorable condition may identify with their poor state and forced oppression or underdevelopment as part of their very own nature, and hate, or fight anyone who attempts to rescue or lead them to freedom or to a better life or a better state, because they will see any rescue attempt as an attack on their nature, since they believe it is their fate, their cultural identity or their 'God's will' for them to suffer and be in that deplorable, unfortunate state or life.

It would seem that the American scientist, Carl Sagan provided a concise and befitting description for such a bio-psychological condition when he stated that: "One of the saddest lessons of history is this: If we've been bamboozled long enough, we tend to reject any evidence of the bamboozle. We're no longer interested in finding out the truth. The bamboozle has captured us. It's simply too painful to acknowledge, even to ourselves, that we've been taken." Carl Sagan is a professor of astronomy and space science from New York, USA.

Again, you can understand why I already pronounced thinking to be the most difficult human activity. I base this conclusion on the undeniable and all too familiar evidence that surrounds us, from family to family, community to community, society to society, nation to nation and continent to continent. All you need to do to see this is just to travel and see for yourself. Many would rather face disasters or even death than think constructively and creatively in modern society and the supporting evidence of this phenomenon is all around us.

Many are too busy playing *"go with the flow"* game or *"the copy-cat"* game to even notice what is really going on around them. Individuals instead of thinking make all kinds of excuses to avoid thinking. A classic example is the millions of citizens of North America, a nation said to be the leader of the free and developed world.

In this named nation above, millions of well-educated and non-educated citizens when faced with domestic crisis or mass murder by American domestic terrorist groups or other hate groups on American soil, just hold hands and sing or march, rage on social media for attention without resolutions, and as history records, such victimised groups have been responding collectively to such injustice, genocidal acts and oppression in their own homeland by the same old ineffective and illogical methods year after year, generation after generation. Only constructive and progressive thinking under the right leadership can solve this seemingly hopeless and repetitive canker.

Therefore, no one in this world seems to take them serious whenever there is an outcry by the same groups in their homeland in the United States of America since they refuse to deal directly with important matters and refuse to change or act even in the face of unthinkable injustice and death. 'What are they thinking?' is often the response of others, looking on and witnessing the plight and distress of these communities within the USA, a country often referred to as the land of the brave and home of the free. Taking this repetitive case in the USA as an example, it is safe to conclude that constructive thinking is not a consideration to the Masses.

The noble prize winner George Bernard Shaw once said that the average person thinks 2-3 times a year, and that he gained an international popularity just by thinking about 2-3 times a week. I guess he is onto something big and just by making these statements he has added confirmation and become a tangible evidence to the above assertions and the importance of engaging in thinking as a human being.

A certain doctor from Kentucky, Dr McFillin after conducting a study in the USA, disclosed that about only 2 percent of the people population think, 3 percent assume they think and the remaining 95 percent would rather die than think. Honestly speaking, which percentage or group would you say you belong to or fall into after assessing yourself completely with no bias or excuses? These are strong condemning conclusions to most of the individuals living today, who make up the majority of the human species except for the thinking few.

Unfortunately, the overwhelming evidence of this entire scenario is what we see all around us, with global turmoil, political unrests, religious and racial conflicts in all parts of the world where there is an established country of some sort. Colin Wilson in New Pathways in Psychology had this to say: "This is one of the most urgent problems for civilised man. He has created civilization to give himself security. Security for what? For boredom? His chief problem seems to be that most human beings need a certain amount of challenge, of external stimulus, to stop them from sinking into the blank stare and blank consciousness of the idiot."

"Most people are, in the most ordinary sense, very limited. They pass their time, day after day, in idle, passive pursuits, just looking at things - at games, television, whatever. Or they fill the hours talking, mostly about nothing of significance - of comings and goings, of who is doing what, of the weather, of things forgotten almost as soon as they are mentioned. They have no aspirations for themselves beyond getting through another day doing more or less what they did yesterday. They walk across the stage of life, leaving everything about as it was when they entered, achieving nothing, aspiring to nothing, having never a profound or even original thought… This is what is common, usual, typical, indeed normal. Relatively few rise above such a plodding existence." writes Richard Taylor, in his book Restoring Pride.

The other things that many also do besides watching tv and playing games is going to sit in a church or some religious gathering, five days out of the seven days in a week and then pursuing avenues that offer quick cash in the form of loans or charity since there is no time left for those who deemed it right to go to church every single day of the week and overlook or neglect their physical life, existence and relations. They do all these things not at their leisure but sadly and unfortunately for them; they engage in these meaningless and acts of vanity at the cost of neglecting their primary and immediate responsibilities as human beings living in a tangible world.

These believers truly and often blindly consider themselves righteous in their own eyes, and believe to be in the right by their measurements and in the eyes of their god they serve, to engage in the practice of building heavenly riches, and to invest in a place they have never been or seen, to become a citizen of a heavenly kingdom in the afterlife, in a mystic kingdom or paradise of which they know not its exact location, a kingdom which they have no evidence to offer in proving its existence.

Would you say it is possible for anyone to have complete trust, faith and belief in such contradictory concepts and such flimsy, empty promises or teachings after carefully contemplating this question among many other similar questions as discussed earlier in the preceding KEYS?

In an attempt to justify one's self, one may claim that "Some people, in no doubt, are born, and destined, to be common, to live out their lives to no significant purpose, but that is relatively rare. Most people have the power to be creative, and some have it in a god-like degree…But many people - perhaps even most - are content with the passing pleasures and satisfactions of the animal side of our nature.

Indeed, many people will account their lives to be successful if they get through them with only minimal pain, with pleasant divergence from moment to moment and day-to-day, and the general approval of those around them. And this, notwithstanding that they often have within them, the ability to do something which perhaps no other human being has ever done. Merely to do what others have done is often safe, and comfortable; but to do something truly original, and do it well, whether it is appreciated by others or not - that is what being human is really all about, and it is alone what justifies the self-love that is pride."

The interesting thing is that some people actually think only if they are faced with catastrophes or life-threatening situations, thus making thinking their last act in desperation.

With humans, thinking in fact ought to have been the very first act preceding any other, and not the last resort after all other options are exhausted and all attempts and everything else has failed. Yet the latter is the order of the day when it comes to the Mass and how they deal with or live their lives. That is why humans as a group face global crisis in almost every part and at every level within existing societies, organisations or nations.

There never seem to be an end to the problems, and the rate at which these problems are growing is faster than we can find solutions to. I wonder what would have happened had they (the Mass - including civil servants, doctors, farmers, teachers and so on) develop that attitude of thinking beforehand. No wonder there seem to be more problems than there are solutions all around the world. Amid all of that is plaguing the world, with the widespread deception, chaos and turmoil, we are still thankfully, because we have a solution to these major global problems.

8.3 Connecting Hearts

Thinking the right thought is as vital to the individual's wellbeing as breathing. Thus it behoves us as humans to engage in thinking, to reason and if it be possible to think and dwell on original thoughts that lives in the creative planes daily instead of passively and comfortable being dragged in life by one circumstance after another. Through the act of engaging in original thoughts, many have helped usher in new and improved technological, philosophical and cultural ages that has made possible the technological advancements we are witnessing all around us today.

As long as we think and dwell on or meditate on pure, edifying, positive, honourable thoughts, we shall never be in want or lack and we will have no use for competition of any form, whether it be mild or fierce competition, healthy or unhealthy competitions because there is nothing at all healthy about engaging in competition. Each time someone claims to educate you or convince you of healthy competition, it is exactly as though that someone is convincing you to try some healthy cigarettes or healthy genetically modified foods as part of your daily routine.

Consider this: an honourable, selfless businessman will not adopt fakery and trickery to make profits at the expense or detriment of others. Again, would any good, morally sound, pure of heart and authentic, philanthropic, selfless organisations or individuals and professionals such as doctors or physicians and pharmaceutical companies engage in the spreading of viruses, carcinogens, sterile vaccinations to infect and murder millions while making great financial profits through the sale of their created antiviral drugs and other medicines and then donating placebos and harmful or expired drugs in the name of 'charity work' or 'foreign aids'.

Only a world full of dumb, deaf and dead (inactive or zombified) people would accept these methods of operations and praise those transnational hyenas and corporations engaging in such practices as philanthropies or heroes and role models worthy of celebration. You have got to be in a non-thinking, unintelligible world or a docile mental state to witness such immorality, wickedness and barbarism, wantonness and nepotistic ways of life daily and accept or act as though all is well or that all will be well in due time. To be in such a world is definitely to be in hell.

If you ever entertained the idea that you have no power or chance to change what is happening then reconsider how that idea or thought got into your head and became your reality, because no organisation or revolutionary, and no nation could have been born or successfully built in an instant.

All things, whether big or small, usually start with one person and then grow with time and effort and organisation and invitation of comrades and members. That is how things are accomplished and not by receiving an idea and worrying or imagining whether it can be done by a single person overnight, before it can be deemed a viable and practical idea. If that was the case, nothing would have been done and perhaps you would not have been born at all. Remember that next time you get an idea worth exploring, before you kill that idea prematurely.

By thoroughly reading and understanding this book, with all the knowledge it contains, you will realise your liberation with precision and certainty in the shortest time as you engage in the matter of life from all fronts as directed here in this book. You cannot fail to become a successful person, though this endeavour may not come easy to some. However, the sacrifices, pain and effort required to become a successful human being as directed here pales and becomes infinitesimal compared to the great benefits and rewarding reality of the successful person you will become. The results will then be clear for all to see as you contribute to a mutually beneficial world.

8.4 Your Greatest Asset Is Your Mind

After your birth, the greatest battle you will ever encounter as an individual is the battle that is waged on your mind. This is an automatic, unprovoked assault and does not require your consent, acknowledgment or awareness in any shape or form. In fact, the less aware you are of this battle waged against the control of your mind, the easier and smoother it will be for your mind to be conquered without the mind getting the fair chance to put up any difficult resistance or attempting to fight back.

The predetermined outcome of this war is for the ultimate control, subjugation or the complete destruction of your mind as the end game if total subjugation or control fails. That just happens to be the order of the day. Just like being born into a war zone. You either fight or take flight and if you are caught in the line of fire, or hit by a stray artillery or a stray bullet, you end up a casualty. And thus the greatest victory you could ever enjoy would be a victory where you take absolute charge and control over your mind and all relating affairs, making subjects of your emotions and feelings instead of becoming a subject of your feelings and emotions.

You can successfully control your mind and achieve greatness, knowing that your mind is by far your greatest asset. The Mind undoubtedly being your greatest asset is also the architect of your life, therefore making it an invaluable asset to have and properly understand and maintain. The good news here is that this asset of great potential and inner power is something you are born with, and it is free!

You own a mind right from the commencement of your life. Your mind is the single most important and powerful part of you as a human being. It is no wonder that the greatest battle waged will be that on your mind, and not in some faraway country, or in the backside of some unknown desert. There is no escaping this.

So in guarding your mind, it is no exaggeration to say that you ought to guard it with all your might and with all your strength. Guard your mind with all assiduousness, guard your mind as though your life depends on it, because it really does.

Your life depends on the welfare and stability of your mind. Now if someone was to come into your home and dump rubbish on your carpet, whether that carpet was old or new, what do you think would happen? Am most certain that majority of individuals finding themselves in such a situation would act immediately along the lines of using either threats, anger, physical assault or a combination of these to force the perpetrator who dumped the refuse on the carpet in their living room to clean it up. And if the threat or assault is convincing enough, you can be sure that the culprit will respond immediately to the request to clean up that rubbish they dumped on the floor or carpet.

Yet many allow and even support others to dump garbage, filth and nonsense in their minds, which is their heart of hearts and the control centre of their life. The Mind is the control centre for all your mental activities, both small and great and also the headquarters where the seat of all significant human emotion lives.

Next time someone starts an unwholesome, pessimistic talk or conversation with you, immediately decline the offer or temptation to indulge in such unwholesome, life-draining activity. Do not compromise in such situations because this is too dangerous for you and a path you needn't take. Many take such a road of compromise and end up in the abyss, never finding their way back to the pleasant side of reality. So do not fall into that trap.

A study conducted by a group of researchers at Harvard University in Human Psychology on effects of words and happiness showed that if an individual was told once, *"you cannot do it"*, that same individual in order to be convinced he/she can do that which he/she was told he/she could not do, would have to be told *"You Can Do It"* seventeen (17) times.

This means for every one negative thought, suggestion or instruction received, it would take 17 or more repetitions of a positive, opposing affirmation or suggestion to cancel out that single negative suggestion or instruction. Only then would that individual's mind be convinced that it can achieve whatever it was told it could not achieve earlier. This is no small task. Thus, if you are to take and act on any advice, let it be something about productive and creative thinking.

Consider the following ancient proverb given by an old African royal priest and philosopher some 20,000 years ago, and you will see that this timeless advice is still relevant and of great value today in our current world. I have given a rough translation of this statement: "whatever is worthy of reverence and is honourable and decent, whatever is just, whatever is pure, whatever is lovely and inspiring, whatever is kind and winsome and gracious, think and fix your mind on them, feed on such as these and strive always for excellence in all your endeavours and remember always to do no harm to others".

8.5 Mind Renewal Precedes Life Transformation

Do you desire a complete transformation? Tired of suffering one defeat and disappointment after another? Are you sick and tired or being sick and tired daily? Are you ready to trade your existing harsh life for a new and better life of success with meaning, purpose, fulfilment, and joy? Do you desire to enjoy success in all areas of your life, from a healthy body to relationships, to financial success, educational success, and more? Is this desire strong enough to where you are willing to sacrifice short-term pleasures or gratifications to achieve the desired transformation? If the desire is not that strong then it means you have not yet gone through your toughest hardships, you are in denial or you are in some kind of a trance or caught up in a spell that is keeping your mind bound or docile.

As there is a way to bind, there is a way to set free or to transform and there can be no transformation, no fresh start or renewal of life without first renewing and transforming your Mind. To do that, follow the prescribed instructions on undergoing an entire mental cleansing and recreation of yourself. That is the only sure way forward to a new life, the only certain way to success that comes with real transformation, lasting freedom and progressive growth.

No legislations or laws, no amount of fasting or praying, no amount of formal education, no amount of singing and marching or chanting can get you to where you ought to be and what you need to be except you authentically engage yourself and mind. Anything else apart from this is just passing time or avoiding the reality before you.

The next question most likely to come into the mind of the reader would be: How do I transform my mind, which I can neither touch nor see? The answer is simple yet not simple enough to be summed up into one short sentence. Thus in the next three to five minutes as you continue reading, all will be clear as daylight and you will see the explanation and instruction on how to achieve this transformation. Whenever you feel the need to re-visit or re-read some or all parts of the preceding KEYS, do so as many times as necessary and do this for the entire book and KEYS within, until you are at peace and in tune with what it is you are reading here.

You are a living, breathing being formed from nature and truth. You have been formed through the collective act of nature and you are only complete in nature and not outside nature, since nature is your original source. Truth is nature and nature is truth. These two are inseparable. Truth here stands for reality and reality is the world around us and that same world out of which you came.

Reality is neither the recreated world by your big media and private advertisement companies we now perceive, nor the reality you were taught in your school days or university days. The reality we are talking about is the one and only true reality which consists of the actual tangible and perceivable world around us. This can be quite confusing or sound strange to many because as it stands, most individuals have unfortunately been completely shielded away from this real reality through subversion, deception and brainwashing from their childhood.

These lies and artificial constructs are spread effectively and made a second reality covering the original, pre-existing reality through large media outlets using constant and repetitive broadcasting of lies (sophisticated lies and simple lies) and OPINEWNS (carefully structured opinions branded as news to the public or the individual). Unfortunately, the masses are, for the most part unaware and mentally susceptible to the ongoing mental assault and subliminal controls, and these strategies have created victims out of the Masses.

Over the years and decades, these deceptions and illusions form a new reality for the Masses (or victims) as it eats into their biochemical beings, and as a result, these victims (the Mass) begin to develop a collective addiction to these stratagems of deception and illusions, resulting in the worldwide social disillusionment, deep-seated-dissatisfaction, chaos, national and international conflicts among many other undesirable conditions of living.

As indicated earlier, truth (nature) therefore comprises many things including trees, water, knowledge and words. Nature as we have discussed earlier, you may begin to realise that not all parts or aspects of Nature can be seen with the human eyes, regardless of how healthy your eyes may be.

A lot of the perceivable parts of nature can be artificially distorted, and this is usually done by others solely for economic profits. The part of nature we are most interested in now is the most basic part, which is the best and most appropriate part to begin our discourse. This most basic part is the observable part of nature from which we derive knowledge and we usually communicate this form of knowledge through the use of words. This is why words are so important.

Now you may understand why words can be used to create new worlds, and at the same time we can use them to make or break people and nations. Words, knowledge or ideas can cause more damage than we give credit to since the words and ideas of individuals in the past have had great positive or negative impacts on living beings over centuries long after the passing away of those individuals who spoke those words or brought those ideas into existence.

There is no punch on earth that can possess even up to a quarter the lasting impact of words and ideas. Sticks and stones may break your bones, but words cannot cause such physical damage no matter how loudly or softly they are spoken. That may be true, but no stone or stick can break a human's spirit. Spoken words, however, have the potential to break the spirit of an individual without breaking their bones or causing any physical damage. Such is the power of words, knowledge, and ideas.

There are positive words and negative words. Positive words are truthful words or utterances and negative words are lies. These are opposites, constantly contending with each other for control and power. You can heal yourself and build a natural mind by feeding mentally on truthful words.

The habitual meditation and visualisation of truth (truthful knowledge/words) leads to the construction of positive thoughts. A saturated cloud of positive thoughts leads to the generation and activation of a positive mind. This positive mind upon further development with more truth being fed into it leads to the creation of desired habits. These new and positive habits are concentrated dynamic thoughts that activates the creative force within you and connects to the Universal Creative Force which results in a transformation by creating a new being, a new you.

This metamorphosis you have just undergone results in the harmonious state or life of success you once dreamed or desired. That is how to do it in a nutshell.

A widespread of this way of life and replication of this process will build great nations and empires. The direct opposite of this process is the creation of hell and the destruction of a human being, the destruction and undoing of an individual and their personality, and continue on this process long enough and an entire nation will be destroyed in the same way, starting with individuals, then families and so on.

By the correct recreation and transformation of your mind, a new dawn arrives. You are reborn, old things have now passed away and all things become new. You may not have physically changed much, although (phenotypical) changes will slowly follow. You are instantly transformed into a new being. You will no longer be subject to or suffer from the old negativity and trickery that caused your suffering.

You will realise that old mental suggestions that once crippled you and threw your emotional state out of balance and harmony will have no effect on the new person you have become, as you have now become immune to such crippling, dehumanising mental suggestions, immune to deceptions and information.

You now see things from a new and higher plane, beholding an entirely new world which was hitherto hidden from view while you were yet bound and docile in an artificially created comfort zone and in a world of illusions and lies. The wonder here is that this transformation makes you aware of a mysterious world and a new form of life you never considered possible.

With such finely tuned awareness, you now have a new understanding of nature and creation, the true understanding that all men and women, and the whole of creation are your friends instead of enemies, that the cosmos is not going against you but is rather for you, and nature itself becomes friendly to aid you in your quest for meaning and purpose in your own life.

You will understand that there is no need for competition and there is no need for you to set yourself against nature or try to conquer nature, for you cannot conquer your source. This newness of life brings radical changes into your life, all fear is eliminated and love becomes your experience, bringing with it awe, appreciation and unspeakable joy among many other good and beneficial things.

What I can do, you can do. What one can do, all can do! We are all born into this world naked and learn to do the things we do, some better than others. We can go on and on with facts upon facts and analysis upon analysis. At the end of it all, the ultimate responsibility to changing your life rests with you and you alone. Get focused on what you ought to do and do it. That is the way.

Renew your mind and grow out of the competition and all the craziness that has been normalised by societies and governments over the decades and centuries. It is a new era and the whole of creation is waiting for you, to take your place as a sons and daughters of the Cosmos, to give your own small contribution to the force of creation, to recreate lives that flow in perfect harmony and synchronicity with the Cosmos.

8.6 Thinking And Worrying Are Arch-Enemies

Think constructively. Do not worry. Do not mistake worrying for thinking because they are different activities on different wavelengths. One is empowering (thinking constructively) while the other is disempowering (worrying). One activity stirs up power from within you while the other saps away power and health from you. So it would be a wise thing to never again mistaken these two activities to be the same. This is the common mistake people make when we talk about thinking and worrying.

When we talk about thinking as a vital part of realising your dreams and enjoying success through the fruits of your labour, many confuse this wonderful and highly spiritual activity of creative thinking with the dangerous, energy-dissipating activity of stress called worrying.

Yes, many individuals go on about their business in life worrying and then making the sad mistake of believing that they are thinking. As a result, they inevitably reach a flawed conclusion that thinking is not for them or that thinking seems to be a stressful, overrated, redundant and ineffective or unnecessary mental activity in their life. That is the tragedy of life; to mis-identify and confuse the act of worrying for the act of thinking. Thinking is constructive while worrying is destructive. So you cannot engage in destructive habits and expect to have a productive life.

Many people go through life without ever experiencing true and complete joy and happiness. This is because they are still holding on to some negative childhood experiences or failures they met in the past. Some can even hold on to a past bad relationship in their primary school days and for the next fifty or sixty years never get married or have anything to do with the opposite sex, after a little fellow who was their classmate at the age of about 6years old told them some hurtful or inappropriate words that messed up their day at that age. From that age of about 6years old, they kept playing those hurtful words over and over and never learnt to let go. What a life that is! This is nothing more than living in the captivity of your recreated negativity or negative experiences.

Emancipate yourself, liberate yourself from those dark shackles of mental slavery, oppression and mental imprisonment and answer the great call of destiny. Life is a beautiful gift so treasure life while you still can. Think your way out of your troubles. Live as much as you can each day. Worry is nothing more than a form of a deadly spiritual poison that leads to another slow acting poison called fear. Thinking can help you produce solutions to troubles you may face or troubles someone may face and thinking can also help you create useful and timely plans that can benefit you individually, or the country or organisation to which you belong.

The only thing worry can definitely produce is stress, anxiety, pre-mature grey-hair, headaches, depression, stomach ulcers and high blood pressure among other ailments. These are the side effects of worrying. Stop worrying daily about your life, what you shall eat or what you shall drink, or about your body, or what you shall wear. It is meaningless and worthless to worry. Since you started your journey of worrying, have you been able to solve any of those problems through that act of worrying or have you improved your physique in the slightest bit? The answer is no, not at all. It is impossible to reap any great and positive benefits from worrying, whether or not you feel it is justifiable.

Each individual has the sole responsibility of controlling his or her own mind. No one can take control of your mind without your support or input. No one can take control of your mental state except by your permission. You can change your mental state to benefit you by your own will, by focusing and exercising your will. Failure to do so will cost you greatly.

Below is a true life story of how an 8year old boy suffering from fatal burns used the power of a determined will to change his entire life and became an inspiration to many who heard or read his story. This report is a real-life story written by Burt Dubin, a well-known public speaker and trainer and published in Chicken soup for the soul book in 1993 by Jack Canfield and Mark Victor Hansen. The story tells the account of Glenn Cunningham, an athlete who was horribly burned in a schoolhouse fire when he was eight years old. Doctors predicted Glenn would not survive treatment and that even if he survived, he would never walk again because of the extensive damage the fire had caused to his lower body.

"The Power Of Determination

The little country schoolhouse was heated by an old-fashioned, potbellied coal stove. A little boy had the job of coming to school early each day to start the fire and warm the room before his teacher and his classmates arrived. One morning they arrived to find the schoolhouse engulfed in flames. They dragged the unconscious little boy out of the flaming building more dead than alive. He had major burns over the lower half of his body and was taken to the nearby county hospital. From his bed the dreadfully burned, semi-conscious little boy faintly heard the doctor talking to his mother.

The doctor told his mother that her son would surely die—which was for the best, really—for the terrible fire had devastated the lower half of his body. But the brave boy didn't want to die. He made up his mind that he would survive. Somehow, to the amazement of the physician, he did survive. When the mortal danger was past, he again heard the doctor and his mother speaking quietly. The mother was told that since the fire had destroyed so much flesh in the lower part of his body, it would almost be better if he had died, since he was doomed to be a lifetime cripple with no use at all of his lower limbs. Once more the brave boy made up his mind. He would not be a cripple. He would walk. But unfortunately from the waist down, he had no motor ability. His thin legs just dangled there, all but lifeless. Ultimately he was released from the hospital.

Every day his mother would massage his little legs, but there was no feeling, no control, nothing. Yet his determination that he would walk was as strong as ever. When he wasn't in bed, he was confined to a wheelchair. One sunny day his mother wheeled him out into the yard to get some fresh air. This day, instead of sitting there, he threw himself from the chair. He pulled himself across the grass, dragging his legs behind him. He worked his way to the white picket fence bordering their lot. With great effort, he raised himself up on the fence. Then, stake by stake, he began dragging himself along the fence, resolved that he would walk. He started to do this every day until he wore a smooth path all around the yard beside the fence. There was nothing he wanted more than to develop life in those legs".

Ultimately through his daily massages, his iron persistence and his resolute determination, he did develop the ability to stand up, then to walk haltingly, then to walk by himself—and then—to run. He began to walk to school, then to run to school, to run for the sheer joy of running. Later in college he made the track team. Still later in Madison Square Garden this young man who was not expected to survive, who would surely never walk, who could never hope to run—this determined young man, Dr. Glenn Cunningham, ran the world's fastest mile! Burt Dubin".

Interestingly enough, this young boy even at such a tender age of 8years had a mind of his own, a different mental state that refused to make the beliefs and opinions of others cripple him for his entire lifetime. Even the opinions of a qualified medical professional did not stop him from recreating his own ideals and seeing it through. He fought all the way and won. He had already showed signs of independent thinking even at that tender age, right before he had entered his teens. Independent, sound thinking without a doubt creates for the thinker a state of positive mental attitude of endless possibility and creativity, regardless of physical, transient earthly circumstances.

Now in relation to the above story you just read, it is a recorded and well-known fact that in February 1934, in New York City's famed Madison Square Garden, this young man, Glenn, who was not expected to even survive the accident he was involved in, after he was told he would surely never walk again after a medical assessment by medical doctors, relied on his own original thought to produce a physical healing in his body that allowed him to walk and then ran a mile in four minutes and eight seconds, the world's fastest indoor mile.

By his achievement, Dr. Glenn Cunningham had set a new world record in February 1934, and his story became an inspiring one for many who witnessed it. Now you could also have an inspiring story of your own to inspire many if you just let go of those fears, worries and doubts and the many layers of false knowledge you have been living by for all these years. Time has come for a positive change, and you could be counted among the heroes and role models who made the impossible possible.

Concluding statement: Free your mind, Free yourself.

CONCLUDING STATEMENTS

"When a silver coin falls into a well, many will look into the well, but very few will dare to go into the well for it."

African Proverb.

All in all, do your best always and be the best you can. Strive to live in perfect harmony and in consistency with your true nature. Someone may have been responsible for your current condition and for making you what or who you are, but now the responsibility for what you ought or need to become is up to you and you have no excuse to fail.

Whenever you get a negative report about your reasons for failing in something, just pause for a moment and remember that it does not refer to or say anything about your potential, or current condition. This is because that report you have received is only a reflection of your condition in the past prior to your engagement in that activity. Never forget that if you choose only to do the easy things in life, your life will be a very hard life but if you do the hard things that need to be done, then your life will be a much easier and happier life.

Although they may disagree strongly on many other things, one thing many great leaders, philosophers, great wise men, prophets and teachers of all ages agree is this: *we become what we think about!* The Roman military leader Marcus Aurelius once said that a man's life is what his thoughts make of it. Thus, by thinking of something, you become something, and equally, by thinking of nothing, you become nothing. This statement speaks truth and reveals the best kept secret of the ages that explains the key to success and the reason for failure in life.

Again, remember that you can never escape from a prison if you are not aware that you are already in one. I would like to share an advice with you and hope this can be of great help to you and those who will listen to you. First of all, let me ask you if you desire to be wealthy. Do you desire to have the ability to provide whatever you need for yourself and become financially independent? If you desire one or all these things which are worthy desires to be pursued, then this following advice is for you. Seek yourself, seek the true knowledge of self and master the ability to use your mind constructively and creatively, instead of sacrificing all you are and all you have to chase money and fame in vain.

Just as I did some time ago, make a resolute decision to acquire the wisdom and knowledge about yourself and what you have to do to get to the highest plane of life. This is your primary responsibility. It is the first responsibility you owe to yourself. This will also be one of the greatest decisions you will ever make in life. Upon this foundation, you will keep developing and keep enjoying from the fruits of your magnificent development day after day, year after year. With this new life, you will be passing down a wonderful legacy that generations after you will come to meet and benefit from, long after you leave this body you inhabit. This is the best investment and pension scheme you can ever engage in, so do not hesitate.

All humans have deep down inside them at least one dream or for some, many dreams they desire to see fulfilled but due to their old crippling thinking habits, or sometimes the complete lack of a thinking habit, they never see the fulfilment of these dreams they have inside. Their dream surfaces in their mind and they quickly push down their dreams with thoughts of doubt and fear, with many excuses such as oh not me, poor me, the entire world is against me, or my family is against me, my teacher said am not good enough, my boss or my spouse looks down on me and other kinds of excuses. With these excuses and other unfortunate or painful life experiences, they brutalise their self-will and determination and cripple their self-confidence. This results in making docile their great mental power which has the potential to easily make those beautiful dreams they have a reality. They allow their dreams to die unfulfilled or to simply stay there in the darkness. They may occasionally fantasise and romanticise about those dreams, without being aware that it is all possible.

The truth of the matter is this: those dreams you desire can actually be achieved. The fact that you may not know how to achieve those dreams at this moment does not mean that it is an impossible dream. You may need to lift yourself up mentally first and become that which you have not been before in order to get the worthy, beautiful dreams you desire to have. You cannot stay where you are and expect those dreams or something better to come your way. You need to go through the transition as described here in this book to become a new person, a new you.

By reading and understanding the principles presented to you here in the 8 KEYS TO SUCCESSFUL LIVING, you can stand on the implementation of these principles to become the new and better you that can achieve those wonderful dreams. Life is a magnificent gift and so make yours count for the better, and you will be glad you did.

ABOUT THE AUTHOR

Finbarr Bassuah M.P.A is a charismatic and knowledgeable individual with a background in Biomedical Sciences. He is a well-travelled speaker and educator, and has a highly rich and diverse experience from working with elite global companies and organisations including Gold Fields Limited, one of the world's largest gold mining firms headquartered in South Africa, the British Council and Chelsea and Westminster NHS Trust Hospital, London.

Finbarr has also worked for the National University of Defense Technology, which is the best military academy for the Chinese army (commonly known as the People's Liberation Army of China).

Instagram: @visionislife
Twitter: twitter.com/ALLGPRINCIPLES
Youtube: tinyurl.com/ALLGREATPRINCIPLES

A

B

C

www.ingramcontent.com/pod-product-compliance
Lightning Source LLC
Chambersburg PA
CBHW022144050726
47590CB00002B/574